•HALSGROVE DISCOVER SERIES ➤

SOMERSET COAST

Rodney Legg

HALSGROVE

First published in Great Britain in 2003

Dedicated to Nick Bowkett of Burnham-on-Sea

British Library Cataloguing-in-Publication Data
A CIP record for this title is available from the British Library

ISBN 1 84114 302 2

HALSGROVE
Halsgrove House
Lower Moor Way
Tiverton, Devon EX16 6SS
Tel: 01884 243242
Fax: 01884 243325
email: sales@halsgrove.com
website: www.halsgrove.com

Printed and bound by D'Auria Industrie Grafiche Spa, Italy

CONTENTS

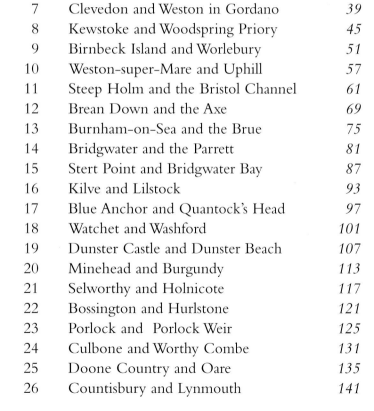

MAP LOCATIONS

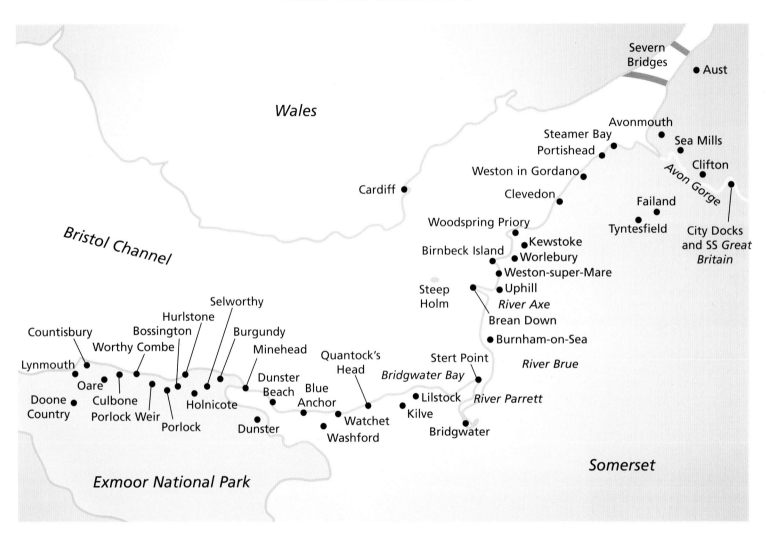

INTRODUCTION

For me it was a triple culture-shock on arriving at Bristol's seaboard from my home near the English Channel. Firstly, the cliffs and beaches faced the wrong way, and secondly, the sea had done a disappearing act, an imitation of that at Southend. Thirdly, when it deigned to return, it was the wrong colour. That was in December 1973 and things could only get better, and did so over the next quarter of a century as I headed this way each summertime weekend, to warden Steep Holm island in the middle of the Bristol Channel.

My western view was to alluring peaks but they remained the scenic wallpaper. My belated personal discovery of the Exmoor coast was entirely due to London accountant Philip Watkins who insisted that its beauty was the equal of Dorset. It took me several years to cross the former sedge-moors of the Somerset Levels to see for myself. I then found he was right, as it is just like a slice of mid-Wales transferred to the seaside. Even the turgid brown waters finally yielded to turquoise and electric blue with an iridescence to match as the Severn Sea merges with the Atlantic Ocean.

The remarkable tidal range of the Bristol Channel became absorbed into my body clock. Its changing moods and character inspired a mixture of wonder and awe as I notched up experiences resembling old newsreel clips from the Battle of the Atlantic. Our 6 miles from Weston-super-Mare to Steep Holm were often against the elements, and often worse for the coming home, yet we were only on the edge of one of the world's great highways. This estuary has linked England and Wales for two millennia, and then the continents of Europe and America, since John Cabot sailed down it to discover Newfoundland and Nova Scotia in 1497. That connection continues with the route taken by Concorde flights in order to give maximum supersonic distance over the sea.

Though historically its own county since 1373, Bristol is more Somerset than Gloucestershire by both proximity and associations. I now stretch the historical 50-mile Somerset coast into its modern reality by absorbing the 10-mile seaboard of the late and unlamented county of Avon. Created in 1974, the administrative aberration hosted a pivotal part of our landscape and lives, with the two Severn Bridges. Visually and psychologically, they and their link roads also unite the lower and upper estuaries, to provide the logical starting point for our exploration. The best is west, however, as Somerset scenery starts well, improves greatly, and bows out with grandeur.

Monumental architecture above the stumps of old fishing stakes

1

AUST AND THE SEVERN BRIDGES

The Severn Way, southwards down the coast from Aust to Avonmouth, links the ancient and modern crossings of the Severn estuary. John Aubrey, in his seventeenth-century *Monumenta Britannica*, describes the 'passage', as a ferry route used to be known: 'Almost opposite to Chepstow is Aust, from whence is a passage over the Severn to Beachley; in Latin it is called *Trajectus*.' New Passage is opposite the English Stones, upstream from Denny Island, and carries a weather-beaten plaque for the crossing made by eighteenth-century preacher brothers Charles and John Wesley who founded Methodism.

Multi-coloured geology on the beach at Aust

Both these points were themselves to be crossed and linked in the twentieth century, first with the building of the Severn Road Bridge to carry the M4 into Wales, north-westwards from Aust in 1966. It opened with a life expectancy of 150 years, with a carriageway 50 feet above the waves that is suspended from twin towers of steel rising 521 feet into the sky.

Then, in 1994, new Severn Bridge was constructed lower down the estuary, westwards from Northwick and New Passage, and took the M4 designation. The original Severn Road Bridge became the M48.

The latter rises from the rich and colourful geology of Aust Cliff, at the other end of which is the Old Passage with the remains of its pier, jutting out through the reed beds to the low-tide line on the outer edge of Northwick Oaze as the mud-flats are known. This disused jetty, to the south of Aust Cliff, still has its rusty turnstile in situ behind a security fence. A second pier, 500 yards towards Aust, carries a single monstrous pylon taking the National Grid over the water and into the Forest of Dean.

Crossed wires of the National Grid and the suspension bridge

'Bob Dylan, youthful with long hair, was the last important person I can remember who caused our generation a flurry of excitement, and there was even a photographer to capture the moment when he travelled this way,' said Glenda Marsh, who had a holiday job in the café at Aust Ferry. That, of course, goes against conventional wisdom which holds that 'If you can remember the Sixties you weren't there.'

Aust Passage now disappears into the reeds

The Boar's Head has catered for travellers for centuries

Pollarded limes in autumn leaf at Aust Chapelry

The other crossing, south of Northwick and Pilning, begins with a widening cutting that was dug by Victorian navvies for the Great Western Railway. After entering the portals of the Severn Tunnel – imperial length 4 miles 628 yards – the next station beyond Severn Tunnel Junction is Newport, just after the sidings to the steelworks at Llanwern. Its chimneys across the water are the principal industrial landmarks of the 7-mile walk that follows which is otherwise dominated by the architecture of engineering and transportation in the coast and countryside between the two bridges.

The Severn Sea, as the estuary used to be romantically known, was the *Sabrina Fluva* of the Romans. It is the confluence of Britain's longest river, which rises from mountain bogs on Plynlimon in the middle of Wales, and is remarkable for a 40-feet rise and fall of the tides. Second only to that in the Bay of Fundy, in Canada, this is caused by the funnelling effect of the Bristol Channel shoreline, accentuated by its open-ended exposure to prevailing south-westerly winds and Gulf Stream currents.

The estuary's cliffside geology took on a new dimension in 2002 when Dr Gordon Walkden announced the discovery of a 2-centimetre layer of greenish glass and quartz with a shattered molecular structure which was dated by Simon Kelle to a thermo-nuclear explosion 224 million years ago. This was the first evidence from Britain of the cataclysmic disaster caused when a 3-mile wide asteroid crashed into Manicouagan in the Canadian province of Quebec. It exploded deep inside the Earth with a force 40 million times greater than that of the atomic bomb dropped on Hiroshima, sending out super-sonic shock-waves and red-hot debris. Ireland and Britain then lay much closer to Canada, before the great shift in tectonic plates split the super-continent. The impact may well have triggered the sinkage and splitting that resulted in the formation of the Atlantic Ocean. A 65-mile diameter crater survives at Manicouagan but on this side of the water it is at Aust that the evidence can be extracted.

THE WALK

The 7-mile walk hereabouts can be joined from many points along the coast but a good option has an inland starting point which is closer for those coming from Bristol or Somerset. Head for a symbol of conventional architecture, the tower of Northwick church – which is otherwise demolished – and the route also brings in the ancient chapelry at Aust. The Boar's Head is at the strategic point in the circuit where you turn southwards and homewards for the final couple of miles.

Approach Northwick by turning east from the A403, which comes off the M5 at junction 18 on the north side of the Avon Bridge at Bristol, being signed to Aust, via Avonmouth and its factory estates.

Park and start in Northwick, which has roadside parking in the vicinity of the 1842-dated Sandford's Charity School – now the local Church of England primary – and Church Farm (ST 559 867).

Set off south-eastwards, crossing the road to the drive through Bob White's Northwick Farm. In 100 yards, in the paddock beyond the buildings, the public path brings you to a stile midway along the right-hand side, in 75 yards. On the other side turn left and follow the hedge to the stiles beside the road in 200 yards. Turn left and head south along the roadside verge for 250 yards. Turn right at the drive to North Worthy Farm, at the start of the slope that rises towards the bridge, and go through the left-hand of the gates.

Keep the garden to your right as you cross the meadows westwards towards the left-hand side of the Severn Bridge. Go through the gate in 250 yards and proceed straight ahead in this field, which has two public paths, following the left-hand hedgerow for 200 yards. You are now heading south-west. In the next field – provided the red flag is not flying

Northwick church is reduced to a tower

Rifle range diversion if the red flags are flying

Plaques to the Wesleys and Terminal Pier, weather-worn at New Passage

– follow the right-hand hedgerow and then cross the grass to an embankment in 300 yards. Turn right along it and pass to the left of a house in 150 yards. Follow the red and white danger poles and keep the military rifle range to your right. The path heads north-westwards, towards Wales, for 500 yards. Across to the left are Redwick and New Passage. Severn Lodge Farm, looking out across Red Ledge and Goblin Ledge, used to be a hostelry where travellers waited for the tide.

If the red flag is flying you must turn right on approaching the red and white poles and follow them north-westwards to the sentry box beside the estuary.

Either way, turn right on joining the coastal footpath. This is the Severn Way and the seaside marshes and flats of Sugarhole Sand and Northwick Oaze are across to your left. The Severn estuary proper begins somewhere between 300 and 700 yards away depending on the state of the tide. Northwick Warth is now backed by the man-made rising ground of Northwick landfill site. Head north-east along the long-distance path for a mile and a half. On reaching the road at Cake Pill Gout, turn left and then right, across a stile at the corner, in 150 yards. The path follows a bank, north-eastwards, with a hedge to your right. Cross the stiles and pastures and then climb a ridge in 800 yards. Here there is a second footpath, striking off to the left and heading north-westwards beside the Old Passage House and the Dower House, but it currently lacks waymarks and the closest practical option is to follow the hedges to the road in 400 yards.

Cross it and walk down to the gap above the Barns. Here you descend to the gates and turnstile of the former Aust Ferry in 50 yards. Turn right along the raised concrete road, which goes as far as the National Grid jetty, in 500 yards. This is an optional diversion, extending in all to about 900 yards, which is strongly recommended for the sensation of looking up to the colossal Severn Road Bridge, rising into what looks like a working model as it carries Matchbox toys with the logos of Asda and B&Q. Take care as you walk along the crumbling under-cliff of Aust Cliff which has a remarkable geology assembled without any regard for colour co-ordination. Clays, limestone and sands of the Westbury beds come in three distinct shades – dull reddish-brown, bright turquoise and gleaming white. Also look out for fossils, such as layers of crushed mussels, but do not venture too close to the bottom of the unstable cliff. The same goes for the bridge, which also becomes a no-go area on the foreshore below, and earlier at high water. It looks awesome as it rises on immense concrete piles from Aust Rock and offshore Great Ulverstone.

Don't turn it into a bridge too far. On returning to Aust Ferry turn left and follow the road north-eastwards, uphill to Cliff Farm and St Augustine's Vineyard, which is beside the Old Parsonage. In 500 yards you pass under the National Grid, beside a particularly hideous pylon. Then in another 200 yards, after Newhouse Farm and Changeways, you will come to the back entrance to Severn View Services.

Second crossing with the new Severn Bridge framing the seaward view

Turn right here, down a leafy track, for 125 yards. Then cross the main road into Aust village. Church Farm is beside the Chapelry of St John. Proceed for 500 yards eastwards to the junction with Sandy Lane. This is between the 1896-dated Zion Chapel – now the Evangelical Church – and the Boar's Head. The ancient hostelry still extends a warm welcome to the bedraggled successors of those coming and going on the ferry route to Chepstow. In our case Paul Cantill and Jayne Leigh not only revived two complete strangers but then remembered us and passed the test again a week later. That was a wet Thursday which hindered completion of a walk originally disrupted by a foul Wednesday. Their message on the door is a lesson to all: 'I've been hanging around here for 300 years, so look after me and close me.' Thinking of those rural public houses, post offices and filling stations that we have lost, perhaps a good addition would be: 'Use me or lose me.'

Opposite the Boar's Head, turn into a raised droveway beside the Foss Ditch, which is signed as the Pilgrim's Way. Proceed straight ahead at a junction with another drove in 600 yards (though remember the other path is there, in case you need to divert back). After another 600 yards fork right through a gate and cross two fields, for 500 yards, to the right of Asnum Copse.

You are heading south-westwards and come to Lord's Rhine. In theory there should be a bridge across it. If this has been replaced, as promised by the highway authority, you can continue straight ahead across the meadows beside Bilsham Rhine to the solitary tower of Northwick's former church in a mile.

English welcome – also expressed in Welsh

If this is impossible, you must turn back across the field to the gate in 300 yards and then bear left, following a second public path in the following field in 200 yards. Turn left and cross the hedgerow in 100 yards to climb through the roadside blackthorn scrub. In the event of backtracking too far, to Foss Ditch, then turn left along the other drove (at the grassy junction mentioned in brackets above). Turn left along the main road, which is the A403, and walk on the verge, to the turning for Northwick in a mile. Here you turn left, following the village signs, to your car in 300 yards.

The Trym at Sea Mills was the Roman ferry point for Wales

2

AVONMOUTH AND SEA MILLS

Portus Abonae – Port Avon of the Romans – came into being on what is now the western side of the Portway around Sea Mills Station and its adjacent streets of Harbour Wall and Hadrian Close. It was the first ferry terminal for crossing the Bristol Channel. The wharf lay on the south side of the Trym tributary at its estuary with the tidal River Avon. Established by the Roman military for supplying the huge legionary fortress across the water in Caerleon, it was built at the end of their equivalent of the M4, in a straight line from Silchester and London. A corn tax, levied on native tribes across the rich chalklands of southern England, provided their basic food supply and the granary for the Second Legion at Caerleon was a vast building, under a roof of heavy red tiles.

The Grand Hotel at Avonmouth

Sea Mills probably began its Roman existence as a fort but soon developed into a large commercial port for the region and its exports and imports by sea. By the end of the first century there was a pattern of streets and the original timber buildings were being rebuilt with stone foundations. Excavation in the garden behind flats at No. 81 Sea Mills Lane, on the other side of the Portway, revealed the ovens of a large workshop. Foundations of a Roman house, with rooms surrounding a courtyard, lie beside Roman Way, opposite a bus shelter at its junction with Portway.

Nearby, in the grounds of former Nazareth House orphanage, evidence of urn burials was found in 1972 which indicated that this was the southern boundary of the settlement, beside its main road. To the east it is easier to define the outer limits of the community as there is evidence of extensive Roman quarrying. These quarries were used for some hasty late-Roman burials which may indicate a piratical attack from the sea. The road eastwards, towards Bath, ran along Mariners' Path, into Pitch and Pay Lane, and then survives as a grassy causeway across Durdham Down. The other road from Sea Mills, to Gloucester, passes Blaise Hamlet and goes through Norton Farm to the west of Cribbs Causeway.

Roman rooms in the grass beside the Portway at Roman Way

Over the hill to the north-west of Sea Mills the remains of a Roman villa lie beside Kings Weston Avenue. Dating from between AD270 and 300, with hypocaust underfloor heating and mosaics, it remained in use through the fourth century and was excavated between 1948 and 1950. It includes a bath-suite with an undressing room and steps down to a cold bath.

Inner wharf at Avonmouth Docks, looking across to Nelson Point

In troubled times, the settlement at Sea Mills would have found itself an exposed and alluring target, which was sufficient motivation for its relocation in the Dark Ages, upstream to what is now Bristol city, where there was protection in depth provided by the snaking mudbanks of the Avon. The same concern for vulnerability rippled through the centuries, until the Second World War, when the Fixed Defences Severn put artillery ptotection across the waters between Brean Down and Lavernock Point. By this time there was a reborn seaward port at Bristol, around Avonmouth Docks which opened on 24 February 1877, after an earlier deployment of heavy cannon had covered the estuary from its twin islands of Steep Holm and Flat Holm.

THE WALK

Avonmouth offers a 9-mile circuit (easily reduced by cheating, either by catching a bus or taking the train back from Sea Mills) that is half through the streets and the rest by public paths. Approach Avonmouth from junction 18 on the M5, along the Portway from Bristol. Park and start from Avonmouth village in the vicinity of the Avonmouth Station, the Royal Hotel, or the Custom House in Clayton Street (ST 514 782). Set off from the level-crossing beside Avonmouth Station, north-eastwards for 50 yards along Gloucester Road. Turn right, opposite St Andrew's Church, and walk the length of Avonmouth Road. Pass St Brendan's Church and cross Portway roundabout at the pedestrian lights in 750 yards. Continue south-eastwards along another 400 yards of Avonmouth Road on the other side.

Then proceed under the motorway bridge into Lower High Street. Turn left in 300 yards, into Kings Weston Avenue, and proceed to the remains of the Roman villa beside the bus-stop opposite Playford Gardens in 700 yards. Then turn right, up Windcliff Crescent, to join Mancroft Avenue in 200 yards. Turn left for 300 yards. Then turn right, up the steps after No. 120, into Penpole Wood where you climb eastwards to Kingsweston House in 600 yards. This four-storey mansion was built by Sir John Vanbrugh between 1710 and 1720, when he was at the height of his fame, between the immense project at Blenheim Palace and another vast house at Eastbury in Dorset. Now the home of John Hardy, and opened as function rooms with a café, it still houses floor-to-ceiling rows of portraits of first owner Sir Edward Southwell and his family.

From here turn right, south-eastwards along the original drive, to the junction of paths to the right of the gatehouse in 400 yards. Turn left, across the footbridge, over the rocky curve at the bottom end of Kings Weston Lane in 400 yards. On the other side there is a public path through a small open space behind gardens, then north-eastwards into higher ground, with woods along the escarpment to the left and old quarries down to the right. In 700 yards this passes to the left of a radio mast and follows the summit of Kings Weston Hill.

The upper green at Shirehampton Park

Here turn right. Look out for a track down through Southside Wood into Ardern Close in 250 yards. Turn left along Southwood Drive and then right down Aldercombe Road in 100 yards. After 500 yards cross Westbury Lane into Hallen Drive. Turn left at the junction, into Sylvan Way, in 275 yards.

After 150 yards turn right into Dingle Way which joins Combe Dale and brings you to Shirehampton Road in 750 yards. Cross into Meadow Way and turn left into Trym Side in 60 yards which follows the River Trym. Turn left into Trym Cross Road, which bridges the Trym, after 600 yards and continue straight ahead across Sea Mills Road for 300 yards. Then turn right in 200 yards, along Branscombe Road and Roman Way, to the Portway in 600 yards. Six Roman rooms can be seen in the triangle of grass to your left.

Turn left along the Portway and cross to the other pavement when – always travel with hope in your heart – there is a break in the traffic. Cross the railway line in 400 yards. Then turn immediately right, down the steps, and right again along the riverside path. You will pass the present and past signal stations of the Port of Bristol Authority – controlling one-way passage through the narrow channel – and turn right to pass under the railway line beside Sea Mills Station, in 400 yards. To your left, behind medieval walling which looks like a section of Hadrian's Wall with reused Roman stone, is a mud-filled harbour. On rejoining the Portway at the bridge over the River Trym, in 200 yards, go left. Turn right in 300 yards, along Riverleaze to the Pentagon in 400 yards, then left into Avonleaze.

Turn right in 100 yards, northwards along a path between Three Acre Covert and the houses of Bluebell Close. After 300 yards cross Sylvan Way and bear left along the lower path across Shirehampton Park which was given to the National Trust by the songwriter and composer Philip Napier Miles in 1922. Beyond, in 1400 yards, the path drops down to Park Road.

Turn left in 200 yards and walk the length of St Bernard's Road. In 700 yards you cross the Portway and the railway line, southwards along Hung Road, to Nibley Road in 350 yards. Turn left in 200 yards, along a public path beside the sports field and then southwards to join the riverside path in 300 yards.

Now head north-westwards, below Shirehampton, with Crockerne Pill across the river from the slipway in 350 yards. In 1250 yards the path emerges from the scrub to pass under the Avon Bridge – carrying the M5 – where you bear right and briefly rejoin the Portway in 300 yards. Then turn left, into Portview Road, and follow it and the railway back to Avonmouth Station in 1350 yards.

Remains of underfloor heating at Kingsweston Roman villa

Molehills and Vanbrugh at Kingsweston House

Brunel's monument, the Clifton Suspension Bridge, was completed as a tribute to his vision

3

CLIFTON AND AVON GORGE

For a dramatic setting, in terms of landscape values, Bristol is up there in the top league with Durham and Edinburgh. It also has deeply historic waters, winding through the Avon Gorge, down which John Cabot and son Sebastian sailed in 1497 and discovered the North American continent. Above all, literally, it has the Clifton Suspension Bridge as a world-class monument to engineer and railway builder Isambard Kingdom Brunel.

Though Brunel designed it in 1830 when he was in his prime, and work began in 1836, the project stopped in 1843 through lack of funds. It was not completed until 1864, four years after his death, and the work was brought to a conclusion as a tribute to his fame. The chains were recycled from Hungerford Bridge across the Thames between Charing Cross and the Royal Festival Hall, which Brunel had designed and erected in 1843. Almost astonishingly for such an impressive structure, there is currently no charge to walk across the Clifton Suspension Bridge, so pedestrians venture onto it free of charge.

On top, at the edge of a grassy plateau, Clifton is a village compared with Bristol proper, with its own open space extending across Clifton Down and Durdham Down, complete with Bristol Zoo as a Victorian specimen in its own right. It is truly a zoological gardens, with exotic animals amid a setting of introduced flora.

The other novelty from a former age is the Camera Obscura, using a 'dark chamber' technique with a lens and a mirror that was attributed to Roger Bacon in 1297, improved by Baptista Porta in about 1500, and remodelled by Sir Isaac Newton. The result, in a lighthouse-sized building in the case of Bristol, is projected down onto a white-painted copper dish which you walk around, turning a wheel to give a 360-degree circuit. It is best to concentrate on the scene of the action and wait for cars and cyclists to cross the Clifton Suspension Bridge. They are strangely three-dimensional, in pastel colours, like a moving colour slide being projected downwards on to a surface 5 feet in diameter.

What follows may sound like an urban walk but it descends into wild slopes below limestone outcrops, among a crop of wild tree and flower species, and offers the chance to see peregrine falcons which have returned to breed. The Avon Gorge provided the only

North tower and a shadow across the gorge (from the south)

City view with the former wharves and spa of Hotwells down below

Western view, across the Avon Gorge, to Nightingale Valley and Leigh Woods

challenging walk that was available in the whole of the West Country at the peak of the foot-and-mouth epidemic in 2001, when all real countryside was closed. Its 5-mile circuit is reasonably demanding, because you descend almost to sea level, and then have to climb back into Bristol. On the other hand the paths are easy to find and to follow. What is the real down-side to the experience is that it is marred by traffic on the Portway which you somehow have to cross – to a pavement on the other side – and then cross back again a short distance later. This particular spot, essential to make a circuit, is as walker-unfriendly as anyone could design. Annoyingly, it is a totally unnecessary hazard because there is a wide pavement on one side of the wide highway and none at all on the other. So prepare to be alert and streetwise in the middle of what otherwise should be applied relaxation.

THE WALK
Approach Clifton up Whiteladies Road, from the city centre, or come via the Clifton Suspension Bridge and either park on the Somerset side or cross and head for a car park.

Park and start by beginning the walk from the Bristol side of the bridge which is an excellent antidote for an adrenalin surge of vertigo (ST 565 731).

Set off northwards from the Bristol side of the Clifton Suspension Bridge by taking the tarred path beside its outer rails, opposite the kiosk, to head away from Clifton. This curves around to the 1829-built Clifton Observatory in 200 yards. Here you can visit the Camera Obscura and Giant's Cave, otherwise known as the Ghyston from one of Bristol's mythical supernatural creatures. It is said to have been a hermit's chapel that gave its name to St Vincent's Rocks.

The Observatory is on one of the banks of a trio of Iron Age forts which commanded the heights on either side of the Avon Gorge. Follow the western bank northwards with the gorge immediately to your left. In 400 yards you return to Clifton Down suburbia opposite the Engineers House. Turn left along the tarred paths down the slope and through the beech avenue to the crossroads in 400 yards.

The Camera Obscura is literally a darkened room

View looking south from the outcrops to tree-covered Burgh Walls

Boundary marker with 'CD' for Clifton Down

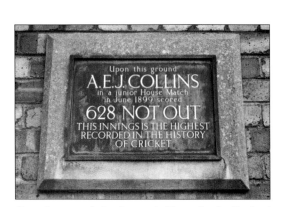

Record score – obviously unsuitable to play for England

Cross Bridge Valley Road into the next section of Clifton Down. Then turn left in 50 yards and follow a scrubby path between the clearings. Keep going straight ahead, towards the sound of the traffic, until the edge of the gorge is visible in 200 yards. The path now bears right, keeping the River Avon to your left.

In 300 yards the road is again to the right and you continue beside it for 500 yards. The road begins to bend to the left after a terrace of houses has appeared on the skyline at Downleaze. Turn left across the grass on approaching a pair of boundary stones for 'CD' (Clifton Down) and 'WD' (War Department). After 50 yards enter the trees and turn left to descend into a gully. In 125 yards you pass a vertical air-shaft for the Clifton Down Tunnel of the Clifton Extension Railway which goes to Sea Mills, Avonmouth and Severn Bridge.

At the bottom, in 200 yards, you emerge from dense vegetation into a patch of level grass beside the outfall of the northern storm-water interceptor, constructed between 1951 and 1962, which drains a network of 75 miles of tunnel devised to relieve flooding in Bristol. The main tunnel, beneath, is 16 feet in diameter. It starts on the River Frome, at Eastville, and runs for 3 miles to discharge here into the tidal River Avon. Without it the city would have been national news for floods in the winter of 2000.

Contemplate how you are going to cross to the other side of the Portway when there is a break in the traffic. The only pavement is beside the Avon. Cross at a suitable moment with both alertness and alacrity. Then turn right, downstream, with the river to your left. Ships, from those that carried the Stonehenge bluestones onwards through the period of Cabot and slavery to the vessels of today, come and go as it fills with the tide.

In 1200 yards, halfway along the fence of the former Bristol & West Sports Field – which carries sale-boards in 2002 – you have to stop again and negotiate the Portway traffic to return to the landward side. There is a narrow gate in the high wire fencing. A public path goes straight ahead across the grass to a similar gate in 100 yards. On the other side turn left, north-westwards, and keep the fence to your left and the Clifton Extension Railway to the right. In 200 yards turn right across the bridge. Then turn right across a stile in 50 yards.

This is Bishop Knoll which was given to the Woodland Trust in 1986. Keep turning left, with Casa Mia to your left, to come out at the bottom end of Bramble Lane in 150 yards. Turn right, up the slope, to the Church Road junction in 150 yards. Proceed up Knoll Hill to the junction in 500 yards. Here, after Greystoke Lodge, enter Seawalls Road.

In 200 yards, at the crossroads, continue straight ahead, up the cul-de-sac between The Avenue and Avongrove Lodge. In 100 yards you go through the gate into Clifton Down. Bear left and head for the buildings to the right of the Water Tower. This is heading eastwards, across a road in 200 yards, and a second road in a further 750 yards. On the other side, in another 300 yards, is Upper Belgrave Road. Turn right, downhill, into Clifton. Scrubland to the right hides the site of extensive medieval lead workings. Follow the road around the edge of Clifton Down to Bristol Zoo, in 500 yards.

Turn left on approaching it, down The Avenue, and turn left at the end in 350 yards. This is Guthrie Road. In the field to the right of the church, converted into flats, A.E.J. Collins in a junior house match in June 1899 scored 628 not out – the highest recorded innings in the history of cricket. Turn right in 100 yards, into Pembroke Road, and follow it for 400 yards. Having passed All Saints' Church turn right into Pembroke Vale.

Turn right and then left in 250 yards, beside the airport-modern lines of Clifton Cathedral, into Clifton Park in another 50 yards. Turn right at the crossroads in 200 yards, beside Vyvyan House, up the next stretch of Clifton Park. Cross to the opposite pavement over the pedestrian crossing beside Clifton High School and walk up to Christ Church and the grassland beyond in 400 yards.

Bear left after crossing Clifton Down Road, from Harley Place, across the park to The Mall and Royal Oak in 150 yards. Turn right in 50 yards, along cobbled Gloucester Street, to the Grapes Tavern and Coronation Tap, in 250 yards. Turn right, beside Bridge House, and then left. Pass Sion Court and Sion Lane. Then cross the grass to return to the supports of Clifton Suspension Bridge in 200 yards.

Human fly defying gravity above the Portway

The Matthew *facing towards America*

4

CITY DOCKS AND *SS GREAT BRITAIN*

Bristol became the first great transatlantic port when John and Sebastian Cabot sailed in the *Matthew* to discover Newfoundland and Novia Scotia in 1497. The Venetian émigré father and son navigators had been authorised by Henry VII to search for the North-West Passage as a short-cut to Asia and ended up in Canada after spending 52 days on Cape Breton Island. Theirs was the first English vessel to land on the American continent. That, however, had not been the aim and a repeat attempt the following year established the scale of the obstacles by surveying both sides of Greenland, Baffin Island, Newfoundland and the North American coast southwards to the 38th parallel.

For seven centuries – from the eleventh to the eighteenth – Bristol, after London, was the busiest and most prosperous port in England. It was pivotal in the 'triangular trade', down to the coast of West Africa and across to the Caribbean, with slaves outward bound and sugar for the homeward third stage. Frigates – light and fast fighting ships carrying between 20 and 44 cannon – were constructed for the Royal Navy by Bristol shipbuilder James Martin Hilhouse. He built 12 warships between 1778 and 1786. The business became Charles Hill & Sons and continued in operation until 1976 by which times it was the oldest firm of shipbuilders in the world. The company motto lives on as the regional catchphrase: 'Shipshape and Bristol fashion.'

Passing time at sea

Bristol's fortunes in the nineteenth century were spiked by crippling competition. The ascendancy of Liverpool was relentless, despite Bristol's attempt at retaining its position by the building of the City Docks during the Napoleonic Wars, between 1804 and 1809. It was also the beneficiary of Isambard Kingdom Brunel's steamship and railway operations. They were in that order. An iron-hulled dredger was his first pioneering ship, the efforts of which enabled his ocean liner, the *Great Western*, to sail from Bristol for New York on 8 April 1838, arriving there on April 23, St George's Day. The railway was still en route with the Great Western Railway from Paddington being completed as far as Bristol on 30 June 1841. The *Great Western* ship was 236 feet long and 35 feet broad. This concept of combined rail and sea travel all the way from London to New York had been suggested to Brunel by engineer Thomas Guppy. So it was the first boat trains set off for Bristol.

Steamship Great Britain *back in the dock where she was made*

Ironically, Brunel's other great steamship that we associate with Bristol – the *Great Britain* having started and now completing her life in the city – actually made her first transatlantic voyage from the Mersey. Stoniers of Liverpool produced her plate. First, however, she had to leave the Bristol dry-dock which had been built for her construction, in 1839, having been found to displace more water than was envisaged. Coping stones had to be removed from the 44-feet-wide lock in the Cumberland Basin in 1844. Then she met her monarch and the people, being inspected by Queen Victoria and Prince Albert in the Thames, in April 1845.

She sailed from Liverpool on 26 July 1845 and arrived in New York on 10 August 1845. The second voyage nearly came to grief when she ran aground in Dundrum Bay, Northern Ireland, on 22 September 1846, and could not be extricated for nearly a year. She was 322 feet long and 51 feet broad, of 1016 tons as her registered weight and 3500 tons burden. State-of-the-art design features included close-riveted wrought-iron plates, bulkheads dividing five watertight compartments, and a dynamic clipper bow.

In terms of size, his third and last major vessel – the *Great Eastern* – was the greatest by far. Launched in 1857, originally with the name *Leviathan*, she was 692 feet long and 83 feet broad, and weighed 12,000 tons registered and more than 24,000 tons burden. Propulsion was by 1000 horse-power paddles and a 1600 horsepower screw.

Meanwhile, the *Great Britain* had transferred to the Australian run. She set off on her first trip with a crew of 138 and 630 passengers seeking their fortune. Gold had been discovered and they were emigrants, taking their own personal bullion with them, in the form of more than £1 million sovereigns. They left Liverpool on 21 August 1852 and Captain B.R. Mathews brought them into Melbourne on 12 November. During the Crimean War she served as a troopship, then went back to Australia for one more trip, and resumed military service in 1857 to take soldiers to Bombay to subdue the Indian Mutiny. Resumed runs to Australia, from 1860 to 1875, included carriage of the first-ever English cricketing tourists in 1861.

Replica of Brunel's dredger which was his first steamship

In 1882, with her engines removed and converted into a sailing vessel, she was demoted to work as a cargo ship. Coal was the outward cargo, down the Bristol Channel from Penarth, via Cape Horn and up the Pacific coast to San Francisco. She returned with wheat. So it was that on 6 February 1886 the *Great Britain* embarked on her penultimate voyage. Battered by a hurricane off the Horn, her Welsh coal shifted in the hull and mangled the masts, but this well-starred vessel had another of her lucky breaks to round off her commercial life of nearly a million miles at sea.

Taken to the Falkland Islands, she was moored off Port Stanley, and utilised as a coal and wool store for the next half-century. On 14 April 1937 she was finally pensioned off and towed to Sparrow Cove where she was scuttled and left beached at low tide. That would have been her grave but for the intervention of expatriate Bahamas millionaire 'Union Jack' Hayward who provided the £150,000 necessary to have her hulk pulled on to the 2667-ton pontoon *Mulus III* and towed home to Avonmouth by the 724-ton tug *Varius II* between April and June in 1970.

On 19 July 1970 that year the tide was just high enough to haul her up the Avon Gorge and then nudge her back into her birthplace, the Great Western Dock, with the Duke of Edinburgh aboard to do the honours. Sir Jack Hayward had already bought Lundy Island for the nation. The other two key characters in the project that has saved the *Great Britain* were naval architect Ewan Corlett and businessman Richard Goold-Adams.

THE WALK

The best starting point for a 3-mile circuit of Bristol Docks is to approach from the A3029 at Hotwells, eastwards along the north side of the River Avon from Avon Crescent and Cumberland Road which are just south of the Nova Scotia Inn at Cumberland

SS Great Britain *partly restored but still with a great hole at the heart of the engine room*

Ferry-boat Matilda *making for Princes Wharf*

Wapping Wharf, looking across to the triple towers of Bristol Cathedral

Basin. Park and start from the western end of Cumberland Road (ST 573 721). Set off northwards to Baltic Wharf. Here turn right, eastwards from the Harbour Master's offices and the Cottage Inn, to Bristol Marina. Then pass between the Orchard Inn and the Graving Docks, to Bristol Diving School and Albion Yard warehouses. Again you are heading for the waterside, along Gasferry Road, to the Dockyard Cafe Bar, which is now the business hub of the Great Western Dockyard.

Here the heritage complex of buildings and quays around the Great Britain include not only the streamship and Brunel's dredger, as reconstructed by Bush & Beddoes of Bristol, but also the home base of the replica of Cabot's *Matthew* built to celebrate its fourth centenary, now on a mooring at Wapping Wharf.

You have come 700 yards and the possibilities from hereon are almost limitless. The city's Industrial Museum is in another 700 yards, on Princes Wharf. Here turn left, northwards across Prince Street Bridge and follow Narrow Quay from the Arnolfini Gallery to Assembly Rooms Lane and King George Place, in 400 yards.

Nora passing Porto Quay with the Cabot Tower rising from Brandon Hill

Graving Dock for the cleaning and repair of ships

Turn left to the Watershed Arts Centre and City Docks Centre between Canons Road and Bordeaux Quay, the vintage import point for claret in England. Millennium Square is across to your right in 300 yards. In another 300 yards pass circular Canons House and walk the length of Hannover Quay and Porto Quay. Then turn inland along Gasferry Lane, for 200 yards, to skirt the ruinous relics of the last of the big stone-built warehouses that used to dominate Canons Marsh.

Turn left at the roundabout, westwards along Hotwell Road to Poole's Wharf in 600 yards. Now turn left, southwards across Cumberland Basin Bridge, in 200 yards. Here bear left, after the Nova Scotia Inn, to return to Cumberland Road in 150 yards.

Riveting became shipbuilding's lost art with replacement by welding in the 1950s

Tyntesfield as a secret world surrounded by its woods

5

FAILAND AND TYNTESFIELD

The National Trust owns two major properties in sight of the upper Bristol Channel. Both have their links with the family fortunes of city magnates. At Failand the Trust was given Failand House with 363 acres of woods and fields by Miss Agnes Fry in 1944, in memory of her parents, Sir Edward and Lady Fry. Sir Edward Fry (1827–1918), a Lord Justice of Appeal, was attached to the international court in the Hague and arbitrated in the disputes between the United States and Mexico over 'Pious Funds' in 1902, and France and Germany after their clash over Casablanca in 1909.

In appearance Tyntesfield could have been the model for Hogwarts School of Harry Potter fame. The author's first sight of the house was in the spring of 2002, after meeting incognito with other members of the National Trust's ruling council to join a mini-bus in the car park of Temple Meads Station at Bristol. Everyone had to sign a promise not to make notes, take photographs, or tell anyone other than National Trust insiders. Now the £24 million acquisition has been secured – the biggest property sale of the year – it is safe to reveal the members' words to chairman Charles Nunnely on first glimpsing the Gothic pile round the final bend of the private drive: 'Doesn't it bring back memories of the first day of term!'

That image was reinforced in a library which had every title a Victorian or Edwardian schoolboy would be expected to read. Envious eyes lit upon a first edition of Charles Darwin's *Origin of Species* which was accompanied by a matching set of all his other lesser works, including a wonderful title that explains the destabilising effects of earthworms on the trilithons at Stonehenge.

It was a warm house, with the pipes recycling chimney heat around the bathrooms, and every one of the 29 rooms was stuffed with family treasures and memorabilia as well as the full kit of servant life downstairs. Family photo albums were stacked in a cellar. Upstairs, the boys' fun room is laid out around a huge billiard table with the latest thing in urinals around the corner. Every time a painting or print had suffered a damaged frame or broken glass it was consigned to join the heap in a lofty roof room. It seemed as if everything had been delivered a century before and that nothing had ever left the building.

Failand House, the former Fry residence, looks north towards Bristol

The Avon Bridge, carrying the M5, from Avonmouth to Portbury

Victorian Gothic at St Bartholomew's in Lower Failand

The far point was a private chapel, the biggest of its kind in the land, with Byzantine-style mosaics and Oxford Movement trappings writ large. It was the best and last time-warp of its kind in the land, established by the wealth of the Gibbs family who imported guano – bird droppings from rainless rocks on the Pacific coast of South America – as fertiliser. The house was designed in 1863 by architect John Norton, with the chapel being added by Sir Arthur Blomfield in 1875, for William Gibbs who died that year. His son, Antony Gibbs, was High Sheriff of Somerset in 1888. He was succeeded by George Abraham Gibbs, MP for Bristol West from 1906, who brought home hunting trophies from across the globe and was created Baron Wraxall in 1928.

George Richard Lawley Gibbs was born the same year and became the second Lord Wraxall, at the age of three, on his father's death in 1931. Lord Wraxall, who died unmarried in 2001, was a practising recluse, or of 'an extremely private nature' as it says in the appeal brochure. As well as preserving the house as a time-warp he let the shrubs and trees grow in the immediate grounds to the house shield it from public view. Lord Wraxall's brother, the diplomat Sir Eustace Gibbs, inherited the title but neither he nor any other member of the family was wealthy enough to buy out fellow beneficiaries and secure the property. So for several nail-biting months there was a real fear that Tyntesfield would be sold and its contents dispersed.

The 6-mile circuit I am suggesting, along public paths along the wooded ridge and back to Wraxall via the valley pastures, hardly gives you a glimpse of well-screened Tyntesfield. For the time being it remains a secret place. The Failand Inn lies a third of the way into the walk and the Battle Axes Inn, at Wraxall, is near the end. Wraxall has otherwise lost its shops though villagers still talk of ninety-year-old sub-postmistress Martha Pike. On reaching that age she was still walking around the parish with the letters on a daily three-hour delivery round. An example to us all.

THE WALK
Approach Wraxall on the B3130, between Long Ashton and Nailsea, and turn north towards Bristol, up Wraxall Hill, at the junction below the parish church. Park and start in the church car park, at the south end of Wraxall Hill, immediately above the junction with the B3130 (ST 494 720).

The Old School at Failand is another prim piece of Victorian architecture

Set off westwards, crossing the road to visit All Saints' Parish Church and its churchyard monolith which must have been inspired by the pagan prehistoric circles at Stanton Drew. It was erected in 1897 to celebrate Queen Victoria's diamond jubilee and also incorporates medieval masonry from the church. The schoolroom was donated to the parish by Richard Vaughan in 1860 and there is a fine marble monument to Captain John Lucas of the Somerset Militia who died in 1817. Tyntesfield memorials record the thanks of 'a grateful parish' to William and Matilda Blanche Gibbs, and tell us that James Nichols, who died in 1891, had been their bailiff for thirty-five years.

From the church gate turn northwards, up Wraxall Hill, and pass Wraxall House and Highfield House. In 300 yards, on the fourth sharp bend, turn right, but only for 10 yards. Instead of passing Rectory Cottage turn left into the trees. Bear right in 200 yards to head east through the dense and rocky wood. You emerge in a field in another 200 yards.

Continue straight ahead, with woodland on either side, and pass gentrified Sidelands Cottages. Beyond, in 200 yards, continue straight ahead at a crossroads of paths. In 400 yards you emerge from the fields and cross the drive above Tyntesfield. Again continue straight ahead, into a narrow gap between stone walls to the left of a yew tree, with a quarry lying down to the left. After 125 yards enter an arable field and continue straight ahead. Follow the power cables and keep the park wall to your right. In 500 yards, down in the corner beyond the lodge, cross a stile.

Bear left in this field, up the slope, north-eastwards towards the centre clump of trees. Beyond the trees the route gradually converges with the road which you join at a gate

Redwood stand of Wellingtonia in Ashton Hill Plantation

and stile opposite Highridge. Turn right, towards the oncoming traffic, and pass Horse Race Lane as you descend to the 1860-dated Failand Inn in 400 yards. In a further 200 yards you come to a crossroads at Oxhouse Lane.

Turn right here, beside Auto Scuderia, along Flax Bourton Road. You pass Jubilee Drive, named for King George V's silver occasion, in 1935. In 900 yards, opposite Clifton Lodge at the junction on Belmont Hill, cross Weston Road to the Forestry Commission access into Ashton Hill Plantation. Bear right on entering the wood, southwards, and then continue straight ahead at the junction in 200 yards. In another 400 yards turn right, after a stand of Pacific coast redwoods, the tall conifer with spongy bark which is known here as Wellingtonia in honour of the Iron Duke. Then descend to a tarred road in a further 50 yards.

This descends to Kingcot Farm, at the corner in 200 yards, and to Gatcombe Mill House in the valley in a further 400 yards. Turn right, north-westwards along a stony drive to the right of the house, and then across a stile beside a gate to pass a second house in 150 yards. In the field follow the former mill leat to a stile in 175 yards which is 75 yards to the right of the stream. In the scrubby pasture on the other side cross quarried hummocks above the stream. You are now heading south-west. In another 200 yards, on joining the sunken track on the far side of the slope, we turn left. Go down it to a point 50 yards from the stream.

Here, in the hedgerow, cross a stile into an arable field. Follow its left-hand side, south-westwards again, for 200 yards. Cross the stream at a humped bridge and cross a field, to the right of a small housing estate, to the road beside April Ash in 150 yards. Turn right, along the pavement, down to the corner in 150 yards. From here follow the main road around the bend to the right to the crossroads in 100 yards.

Turn left along Station Road, towards Flax Bourton, to the corner opposite Mill Farm in 300 yards. Turn right, through the gate into an arable field, to head north-westwards towards the woods above Tyntesfield. Cross the middle of this field and the next, with the main road across to your right. From the third field, in 500 yards, the path begins to converge with the road and joins it at gates on other side of the fourth field in a further 500 yards.

However, instead of going on the road, turn left and follow the conifer hedge to the left of the drive into Gable Farm. You are heading westwards. Around the corner, in 200 yards, cross a stile into the field. Now bear right, for 50 yards, to a stile a short distance

Dereliction at Watercress Farm

to the left of the corner of the field. Cross the muddy green lane and enter the field on the other side. Follow the right-hand edge, to the track at Watercress Farm, in 200 yards.

Turn right along its farm road and then left across the stile into the field in 50 yards. Bear right, heading for the church tower, north-westwards to the fence-bars in the hedge in 100 yards. Keep heading for the tower, to a gate onto a track in 200 yards. Turn right, and then left into the next field, in 30 yards. This is another arable field where you bear right, once again heading north-westwards, to the gate in the hedgerow facing you in 200 yards.

Proceed straight ahead across this field to the gate beside Hazel Farm in 250 yards. Here turn right, along the farm track, and then continue northwards up the grassy slope in 50 yards. Bear left on the ridge, above the buildings, to a stile on to the road in 200 yards. Turn left, into Wraxall village, passing the Battle Axes Inn and following the road to your car, beside the churchyard in 750 yards.

Visiting vegetarian – your author – makes friends with the livestock above Portbury

Seaside town, with Portishead as a spa, from Woodhill Bay

6

PORTISHEAD AND STEAMER PIER

Work in progress at the start of the new millennium is transforming the eastern side of Portishead from derelict docklands into a marina, in a housing sandwich which will comprise a total of 2500 new homes. Meanwhile, though currently sealed off behind barriers, it is a landscape of industrial archaeology and redevelopment. This is typical of Somerset's entire extremity where King Road anchorage in the Bristol Channel has mushroomed into a succession of docks, past and present. Walking is possible, legally that is, in three bursts – with the current offering being at the western end. The great basin of Portishead Dock is the break that prevents progress up the estuary.

Next comes older Portbury Wharf, where there are rights of way for half a mile, but then there is the colossal modern interruption caused by Royal Portbury Dock, where notices deny any public access, followed again by a mile of estuary path up the River Avon, opposite Nelson Point and Avonmouth.

It is sad that such an interesting and busy working landscape, with so many ships loading and coming and going, is denied to us by a mass of chain-link fencing. Places such as Poole Quay have managed to come to terms with people and commerce for centuries but having such a mix near Bristol seems anathema to the port authorities. One wonders what they get up to in secret.

As it is, one must retreat down-Channel to Portishead, where footpaths and roads run the length of the sea front. It also has prolific notices proclaiming the history of this coast. Notably, John Cabot sailed past Battery Point in 1497, on his way to North America. As for the discovery of Portishead, this dates from the establishment of the 1830-dated Royal Hotel, which in its day was high fashion. It still has an impressive dining room and stained glass but the outdoor facilities have vanished. There are few traces of the cricket field, croquet lawn, and quoits court.

To the west, towards Battery Point, the City of Bristol had sponsored an extensive provision of public leisure facilities in the 1820s. These included boardwalks, for fashionable outings and picnics, and reading and smoking rooms for indoor enlightenment.

No entry at the end of public access for the time being

Spa offerings were also incorporated, with plunging baths at the Saltings, seaward of Woodlands Road.

Steamer Pier might have been so much more, as Isambard Kingdom Brunel planned to have his giant *Great Western* liner embarking here, into King Road, for New York. The Royal Hotel would have been the reception centre.

Any residual elegance was overshadowed and engulfed in the twentieth century by massive coal-fired power stations of the Central Electricity Generating Board, strategically sited opposite the South Wales and Forest of Dean coalfields. All this was doomed with the burial of King Coal, emission controls, and development potential of a site inherited by Powergen, the privatised successors of the state-owned electricity industry. As for the shipping, that had already moved eastwards, to the new Royal Portbury Docks, and leisure and housing were the obvious alternatives, to some controversy locally.

Offshore, the view is across to Caldicot and the two Severn Bridges, the far one of 1966 and the nearer profile being the second Severn crossing of 1994. It is an interesting 2-mile walk with the promise of a better 3 miles emerging in the near future.

Channel lighthouse, a metal structure, on Battery Point

Portishead Dock after clearances, from the ancient fort in East Wood

THE WALK

Approach Portishead on the A369 from junction 19 on the M5. Park and start on the sea front at Portishead, in Esplanade Road, or in the parkland near the Marine Lake (ST 463 771). Set off north-eastwards along the Esplanade, with Woodhill Bay and the Bristol Channel to your left and the lake and tennis courts to the right. Further along, to your left, pass the lighthouse, a squat, metallic, automatic structure, and offshore Denny Island. Also pass the swimming pool and footings of wartime gun emplacements, on Battery Point.

This was, reputedly, a Roman signal station, revived in Elizabethan times, for the Spanish Armada. Notices credit its Second World War finale to the Home Guard, but in fact it was operated by professional gunners, being Royal Artillerymen of the Fixed Defences Severn, who also garrisoned the islands of Steep Holm and Flat Holm after their fortification in July 1941.

Cross the grass into Eastwood Nature Reserve. The woody and rocky outcrop conceals the traces of an Iron Age stone-banked fort, dating from 300BC to the time of the Roman invasion. Avoid the tarred roads, and instead cross the top of the wooded ridge along a public path, eastwards for half a mile. It brings you to the Royal, built as the elegant Royal Hotel in 1830, which still makes the area fashionable. Your walk then continues down the steps, beside the former Harbour Master's House, to Steamer Pier. Masses of visitors used to pour ashore at this point, from Bristol, Wales, and southern Ireland.

From here, at the time of writing, you have partially to retrace your steps, though this time passing the frontage of the Royal and continuing along Woodlands Road, passing the 1957-built viewing point, which was an unloading point for the building of Power Station B, above its 9-inch diameter, third-of-a-mile-long, cooling culverts. Houses seawards along the road are the conversions and successors to the reading rooms and plunging baths of the Saltings.

Rocks at the eastern end are Pennant sandstone, a building material with calamite plant fossils of the Upper Carboniferous coal age of 300 million years ago. Westwards the geology is black rock dolomite, of the Lower Carboniferous warm-water seas of 350 million years ago. As for the alternative route back into Portishead, as the derelict industrial area of the former Powergen works is cleared and replaced, look out in the future for a very different waterside path linking Steamer Pier and the next generation of yacht berths with Portishead town. You will then be able to head south-west, in a direct line with the tower of the parish church, not that you will be able to see it any more.

Time-warp view of Portishead Docks in transition from port to marina

Imposing facade of the 1830-built Royal Hotel

Walton Castle – fortification or folly? That is the question

7

CLEVEDON AND WESTON IN GORDANO

Is it a castle, or is it a folly? Walton Castle looks the latter, like a gloriously positioned eighteenth-century extravagance, but residents of Clevedon and Walton in Gordano think otherwise. They are supported by John Collinson, writing the county history in 1791:

This building is of an octangular form, having a round tower at each angle, and an embattled wall between each. In the centre of the area stands the keep or citadel, which is also octangular, and has a small turret of the same shape on the south-east side, rising above the rest of the structure; the roof and floors are fallen in, and no use made of any part of the castle except a small portion of the ballium, which serves as a dairy for the tenant of the neighbouring farm.

Collinson notes the Poulett arms over the doorway of one of the round towers, and the 'castle camp' argue that Lord Poulett built it, as a fortification, in 1615. He chose the site because of its commanding location at the southern end of the ridge overlooking Clevedon and Ladye Bay, watching over Bristol Channel shipping, on earthworks that probably date from the Iron Age. Whichever is the case, it is a scheduled ancient monument, but the compilers of that list have covered their options. Instead of including it in the 'Castles and Fortifications' category, Walton Castle appears in the miscellany, among 'Other Secular Sites and Buildings'.

To bring Collinson up to date, it should be pointed out that these days it is far from ruinous, nor ivy-clad. Indeed, it is not only well restored, by Martin Sessions Hodge in 1980, but is an example of architecture whose time has come again these days; sadly, when for privacy and security well-heeled Englishmen want their homes to be castles, this is not alone in being excluded from the visiting menu. The same applies to two of the three churches passed en route in the course of a 7-mile walk from Clevedon. That at Walton in Gordano is the welcome exception. Likewise the two public houses, but that was down to the wrong time of day, though beware of the two post offices marked on the Ordnance map because one has been subsumed by modern housing and the other is now the Old Post Office.

Such is the way of the world but the surprise when this walk was being researched on a dehydrating day in mid-August was that the holiday coast was closed. No sign of a café

Mis-spelt rocks, with the message on Ladye Point, with Clevedon Pier in the background

or ice-cream van. Neither did the couple of caravan camps offer a public face. Safety fencing keeps walkers put, having been placed there to stop children coming to grief on the cliffs, or in the strongly tidal waters of the Bristol Channel. It can still be a worthwhile exploration, however. The old mariners' path from Clevedon to Portishead is rough and rugged, but passable again after recutting by North Somerset Council's path team – not, it seems because they realised that this walk was about to be documented but because of complaints not a million miles from Walton in Gordano and its parish councillors.

Inland, via an unavoidable close encounter with Portishead suburbia, you can escape to a dramatic ridge of wooded hills with wild common-land nature reserves and the villages of Weston and Walton tucked into folds of the Gordano Valley. It is the far north of historic Somerset coast and countryside; the last green wedge between the shipping and the motorway.

Tidal flow smoothing Backhill Sands in the Bristol Channel

THE WALK

Approach Clevedon on the M5 or B3130 and find the B3124 which brings you into Walton St Mary. This is the northern suburb of seaside Clevedon. Park and start either side of St Mary's Church, in Bay Road or Channel Road (ST 409 727).

Set off along Bay Road – crossing Castle Road if approaching via the church – and follow it to Ladye Bay. Go down the steps about 50 yards before the end of the public road and then turn right along the cliff path. Glance back from Ladye Point for the classic view of Clevedon's Victorian pier. Offshore, beyond the rocky kelp beds, are Backhill Sands. Your direction is north-eastwards, heading up-Channel, with Wales across the water. The steelworks of Newport and Llanwern are particularly conspicuous. In a mile you come to Pigeon House Bay and the radar scanner on Culver Cliff. The signal station itself dates from 1913. Here you will see rock pools and ravens. Pigeons are on the peregrine menu; it can be a lively place.

Keep straight ahead between the caravans and the cliff at Charlcombe Bay. Next is Charlcombe Wood with resident green woodpeckers. Around the headland can be seen the military bunkers of Redcliffe Bay, defending a caravan camp behind, but in limbo since the Cold War. The public path is seawards of the security fence. Denny Island is the offshore rock, with the Bedwin Sands stretching up-Channel to the second Severn crossing. Next is Geoffrey Stibbs's eightieth-birthday seat, dated 1995, overlooking scrubby National Trust cliffs.

About 200 yards after this seat turn right, south-eastwards, uphill between two garden fences to emerge on the road between bungalows No. 24 and 25. Proceed straight ahead, up Waterside Park, and turn right into Hillside Road at the junction facing No. 79.

Keep following Hillside Road around its zigzags, with the final leg bringing us to the Ship public house beside the main road (having made sure you turned right at the junction with Pembroke Road). Turn left along the main road, for 100 yards, and then turn right. Walk straight along Valley Road for 500 yards to the corner after Weston Lodge Farm.

Continue straight ahead, southwards along Blackberry Lane, which is a public footpath. You pass Down Cottage and Brockley Cottage. The path then continues southwards, to cross the wooded escarpment at Middle Hill Common. Keep straight ahead, following the power lines down towards the elevated motorway – the M5 – on the other side of Gordano Valley. The slope is botanically lush and insect-rich.

Military bunkers overlooking Redcliffe Bay

Gordano Valley seen from flower-rich Middle Hill Common

Towards the bottom fork right, along a ferny deep-cut track, which carries horseshoe-symbol indicator posts and descends into Weston in Gordano. The path becomes Hill Lane with the characterful Old Thatch on the right. You emerge in the main street, the B3124, opposite the White Hart.

Turn right, westwards, to Court Farm House, the Village Hall, and Parish Church of Saints Peter and Paul. Proceed beyond the village, walking towards oncoming traffic, to the second field on the right. Here turn right and walk up to the edge of Weston Wood in 200 yards. Now turn left, keeping the trees to your right and valley to the left, to cross a stile into the following field and proceed westwards to its far right-hand corner in 600 yards.

Turn right, into the scrub, and cross the stile. Then re-climb the escarpment, north-westwards to Common Hill Wood. In 250 yards the path turns left and is signed for Walton Common. You are now heading south-west, emerging from the darkness of Common Hill Wood in 700 yards, into the open grassland of its common, which is covered with Iron Age hut-circles, field systems and a stock compound. It is now a local Wildlife Trust nature reserve, leased from landwner Sir William Miles, whose predecessors lost a High Court action in 1892, which upheld the parishioners' rights of recreation against an attempt at enclosure.

Walk straight ahead across the hilltop where insects now have a higher profile than the archaeology, with a remarkable series of anthills. Bear left on the summit, south-westwards into the scrub, where you descend to a badger sett in 500 yards. Take care to manoeuvre around the holes. Beyond them, at a woodland crossroads of paths just before a prominent spindle tree, turn left and follow the edge of the common to the right of Hackswood House in 100 yards. Emerge from the trees at a stile into the fields beside Walton in Gordano. Proceed straight ahead across the stiles to the main road, beside the left-hand house, in 200 yards. If you fail to find this descent into Walton, and continue on the main path for 350 yards, you will emerge instead at the northern extremity of the village, and turn left to walk down to the church in 500 yards.

Presuming, however, that you are on the main road, turn right and then right again at the Cross Tree – an oak – into Walton Street. In 150 yards turn southwards, into a passage between the Old School and the garden wall of the Stable House. The school has its dates, from 1816 to 1932, on a plaque for its 1985 conversion. A public footpath goes through St Paul's churchyard. Pass to the right of the tower. The clock was installed in 1897 to mark Queen Victoria's diamond jubilee. It was modernised in 1995 in memory of Bessie Weeks.

Highways and fairways where public paths cross the golf course on Castle Hill

Bear right after the tower through the Barrow family memorial gate. A grassy path heads south-west, beneath specimen trees between the fields and the Manor House garden. The footpath then continues westwards, straight ahead through the wood, for 150 yards. Next is a corridor across the golf course. 'Beware of golfers' the notice warns (only their balls, one hopes). Beyond, you enter the safety of Rock Wood and bear left, south-westwards, for 200 yards. Then follow the track as it swings right and climbs through the woods of Castle Hill in 300 yards.

Towards the top you enter another fairway and fork left at the junction of tracks. Then continue straight ahead, ignoring a pointer to the next tee, towards the castle and (or) folly. It enjoys a view worth fighting for and is surrounded by the sweetest blackberries in Somerset. The public footpath joins the tarred drive below the green to the right of the castle. Pass the gates to Walton Castle and follow the road, south-eastwards, down into Clevedon. Turn right on reaching Castle Road to complete the descent into Walton St Mary.

Kewstoke Rhyne and the monastic buildings at Woodspring, with the tithe barn at the centre

8

KEWSTOKE AND WOODSPRING PRIORY

A combination of Landmark Trust and National Trust ownership opened up a circuit of paths in a coastal corner of the county where the public rights-of-way do not otherwise join together as a usable network. The former body, founded by Sir John Smith, pioneered up-market self-catering accommodation as a novel means of saving endangered architecture, with the result that a rare collection of monastic buildings in the marshlands between Weston and Clevedon is now available for holiday rental.

Woodspring Priory was founded by William de Courtenay, early in the thirteenth century, as a chapel to Thomas à Becket, the martyred Archbishop of Canterbury. It was handed over to the Augustinian order, whose canons were popularly known as the 'Black Monks' from their habits, who would have as their most famous initiate one Martin Luther who defected to start his own Church. Meanwhile, at 'Worspring' as it was known, the buildings had been expanded by the fifteenth century into a full-sized church, a seven-bay tithe barn that is 127 feet long, and an infirmary.

Woodspring Priory, approached from across the wetlands

The last prior, Roger Tormenton, surrendered the monastery to Henry VIII's commissioners in 1536 but the buildings would be more fortunate than most and survived largely intact, as the home of the Smyth-Pigott family, until a fire in 1876. This destroyed the nave roof and the main part of the church was left in ruins. Decorated encaustic tiles were dug up from around the site of the high altar in an excavation of the chancel foundations in 1885. Otherwise, the medieval buildings have survived remarkably well, and enough remains to piece together the main themes of the religious life.

Kewstoke was known as 'Chewstoke' in Saxon times. Local tradition also gives it a direct link with monasticism. St Kew was said to have been a hermit living in a cell that was reached from the parish church by the Monk's Steps up Worlebury Hill. These and the Woodspring setting have been reunited again through the accident of National Trust ownership which now safeguards key elements of the hilly landscape on either side of the broad expanse of Sand Bay. Monk's Steps, comprising 2 acres, were given to the Trust in 1936. Sand Point, the 32-acre headland, followed in 1964, as the gift of G.F. Burrough. The ridge to the east, around the bay of Middle Hope and across to the estuary at

Sinking sands displacing a wartime pillbox at Sand Bay

Danger signs in the gorse above apparatus awash on the shore

Hucker's Bow, extends to 189 acres. It was acquired through various donations and Enterprise Neptune funds in an ongoing project to safeguard the remaining unspoilt shoreline.

THE WALK

Including a monastic diversion, the 6-mile route is along mainly firm paths but there is a potentially muddy section in the vicinity of Kewstoke Rhyne. Approach Kewstoke from Worle, on the northern side of Weston-super-Mare, and then drive northwards for the length of Beach Road, beside Sand Bay. Park and start in the National Trust car park to the right of the toilets and turning circle at the end of Beach Road (ST 331 659).

Set off southwards, away from the headland, but do so by walking beside the salt marsh and sand dunes, rather than following the road. Keep the sea to your right. Steep Holm is the English loaf-shaped island out across the water with Flat Holm being its Welsh sister to the right; it is the southern-most extremity of the principality. Sample some fleshy-leaved scurvy grass as a natural vitamin supplement. There are 1940-built anti-invasion pillboxes in the dunes seaward of Holm Cottage, Sandpoint Farm, and Swallow Point Park.

In a mile leave the beach and turn inland, crossing Beach Road to Sand Farm Lane, which is 400 yards north of the Long John Silver public house. You are now heading east, along a public footpath into low-lying pastures immediately beyond Sand Farm, in 250 yards. Here the path is channelled into a fenced corridor between paddocks. Then follow the hedge and cross a footbridge in 250 yards.

Turn right on the other side and go through the eastern hedgerow at the next footbridge in 125 yards. Continue straight ahead across the following rhyne (the Somerset name for a ditch) in 50 yards. Cross a succession of former strip fields, each 10 yards wide, with bulrushes colonising the ditches. Go through the gate in 150 yards and pass under the power line to the next stile and gate in another 150 yards.

Continue to head east, with the tower of Woodspring Priory to your left and the wooded Worle hillside to the right. In a further 150 yards, at the kink in the hedgerow, we go through a gate and then bear left, to cross Kewstoke Rhyne in 50 yards. Proceed straight ahead, into the double-hedge green lane, where the author found frog tadpoles in its muddy grey-clay puddles one spring. Their survival depended upon yet another wet summer. In 600 yards you reach Collum Lane.

Turn left, northwards along the private road to Woodspring Priory, passing the Landmark Trust board. Re-cross Kewstoke Rhyne and come to the parking spaces for Woodspring Priory in 600 yards. Here there is a 200-yard diversion, straight ahead along the path to the left of the road in front of Coronation Cottages, and then turn right through the kissing gate into the boggy meadow. Bear left to cross the stream and then pass to the right of the infirmary. Its south wall incorporates the remains of a spiral staircase, showing they were once both outer and upper rooms. Inside, the existing stonework is visibly damp and green, with plenty of evidence of post-medieval subsidence. Next, to the left, you can enter the tower section of Woodspring Priory which includes a magnificent room ('remove muddy footwear') furnished by the Landmark Trust as an example of the lifestyle you can expect in their holiday accommodation. Everywhere there is a wealth of beams, stone carving, and museum cases stuffed with history.

On returning in 200 yards to the farm junction to the south of the parking place, turn towards the modern farm, keeping it to your left. Go through the big steel gate and proceed along the unpaved road, eastwards to the National Trust car park in 350 yards.

This is Hucker's Bow, where Kewstoke Rhyne flows into Woodspring Bay. Climb the embankment of the sea wall, then turn left, but then ignore the next gate to the left

Spiral staircase, the last relic of two outer rooms, above and beside the monks' infirmary

Up Channel, looking across Woodspring Bay, to Clevedon

Holding water, if not quite as the designer intended, beside the River Banwell

and the signs for Sand Point. It is far more interesting to continue northwards along the causeway, into scrubby grassland to the left of the salt marsh beside the River Banwell.

In 400 yards, on approaching the pier, bear left and go up the slope to the wall and fence. Keep this to your left as you proceed northwards for a further 150 yards. Then turn left across the final stile before you reaching the military fencing. Turn right here, cross the access road, and keep the Ministry of Defence compound to your right. Notices warn that if the red flags are flying you must expect explosions. These are offshore, where mines and demolition charges are wired to low-water scaffolding. Though it might seem rather odd to test munitions in the turbid tidal waters of the Bristol Channel, there is a logic as the brown sea then recedes by an almost world-record 40 feet in depth, so that fragments can be recovered and blast-patterns observed.

In 300 yards, at the top of the gorse-covered cliffs, turn left and head westwards. The Channel and the coast of South Wales, at Newport, are now to our right. There is no particularly well-marked path but you have a general freedom to roam across these National Trust sheep pastures. Within a patchwork of relatively recent stone walls there are numerous traces of the patterns of an Iron Age field system to be seen across the limestone downland.

These ancient banks bring you to a small bay at Middle Hope, managed as a nature reserve, in a mile. From here follow the path above the shore for just over half a mile and then cross the final stone wall into the rocky promontory of Swallow Cliff and Sand Point. Continue to follow a right-hand option, for 800 yards, towards the offshore islands of Steep Holm and Flat Holm. The latter has the lighthouse. Southwards, the coastal landmarks are Birnbeck Island with its Victorian pier, and Brean Down beyond as the next National Trust headland.

Observe the geology towards the extremity of Sand Point. Beneath the stonecrop and maritime flora the underlying strata are clearly visible in a tilted plane, upended at 45 degrees, with the angle lifting from south to north. This is the same carboniferous limestone as at Cheddar Gorge and in the Mendip Hills. Having just about reached the western tip of the peninsula turn around and climb the main ridge for your return path. Take care as it is stony and worn in places. In 700 yards it brings you to a mound which is said to be the remains of a small Norman motte-and-bailey castle. The stones and bricks, however, are evidence of a demolished Second World War pillbox.

Next, in 100 yards, are the lesser traces of Bronze Age bowl and disc barrows below and to the right of an Ordnance Survey triangular pillar. From here bear right, south-east-wards down the path into the scrub, to a gate in 200 yards. In another 100 yards you pass the toilets and return to your car.

Conservation grazing as the flock moves into action

Approaching from the south-west, towards Worlebury Hill

9

BIRNBECK ISLAND AND WORLEBURY

The first Somerset book to come into the author's possession was a fourpenny pamphlet by Dorset dialect poet Robert Young on *Rabin Hill's Excursion to Weston-super-Mare* to see the opening of the new pier which took place on 5 June 1867. Much of it concerns his rambling railway journey, via Templecombe and Glastonbury, from where he sends a telegram to establish that he has left his umbrella at Sturminster Newton. On arrival at Highbridge, in the rain, he feels he has 'a come to t'other end ov our nation'.

The end of the line is Burnham Station from where Mr and Mrs Hill walk to the jetty to catch 'the saucy little' *Heather Bell* which 'is quite frisky on the ebbing tide'. This 'be the ship for Super-Mary' but poor Mrs Hill is 'poor an' trembling by the water's side'. She is to suffer in the 'wind and watery strife' as they leave Bridgwater Bay. Birnbeck Island also presented a dismal prospect:

Looking up at the structure designed by pier architect Eugenius Birch

> The tide wer low, the rocks were bare,
> The coast looked ugly to the eye.
> 'O take I back,' zed Mrs Hill,
> 'An' in the ship do let me die.'

She is carried piggy-back to the shore and has to climb the rocks on her hands and knees. Slipping back – 'ther clothes in such a smatter' – the pair eventually climb to the top. They appear at the seaward end of the iron pier as 'dree passons zide by zide' lead the procession across the timbers from Worlebury. The three parsons shower God's 'choicest blessing' on 'this great work'. Master Piggot, who had laid the foundation stone at the start of the project, stands 'so straight an' smart'. Below, the Burnham lifeboat is 'dancing on the restless waves'.

Rabin is sardonic: 'I be so glad I come to Weston 'vore I die.' Mrs Hill admires 'its perty gierdens' with 'flowers a growen everywhere' in 'rocky work, an' slopen banks – 'Tis paradise, I do declare.' It is only a short visit before their repeat experience of being nearly 'drownded':

What happened on the journey back,
It would be needless here to tell.
But when at Burnham, Rabin zed,
'Good-bye, var ever, Heather Bell.'

Burnham was the base for the local rescue vessel until the building of the lifeboat station on the south-east corner of Birnbeck Island in 1882. A D-class inshore lifeboat replaced the larger conventional craft in 1966 but a major drama followed on 12 April 1969 when the Barry Dock lifeboat (ON 806) – visiting as a relief vessel – was torn from her mooring in a violent storm and wrecked. There was no one on board. Ships at anchor off Weston are exposed and vulnerable to gale-force winds with a tidal surge.

Birnbeck's promenade deck was constructed by Eugenius Birch, grand-master of Victorian pier building, in an elegant straight line from Prince Consort Gardens to the island. It stretches 1040 feet. A 300-feet second pier, Meccano-like in steel, was attached to the north side of the island in 1905 for paddle-steamers from P. & A. Campbell Limited and the Barry Steamship Company.

Lifeboat station and the island of Steep Holm

Birnbeck's promenade deck disappearing into the sunset

Birnbeck Pier became known as the Old Pier after the opening of the Grand Pier in 1904 though the latter is now for the end-of-the-pier show rather than practical boating. For more than a century Birnbeck Island and its Paddle Steamer Bar saw regular business from Welsh miners and steelworkers. The Second World War brought its excitements, with requisition of Birnbeck Island by the Miscellaneous Weapons Department, which developed the ship-launched anti-submarine missile Amuck. This went into service with the Royal Navy, as did the rocket-launched Expendable Noisemaker which was put into production as a ship-towed decoy to lure German submarines and acoustic torpedoes from their intended target.

Dereliction, after sections of ironwork rusted beyond repair, forced the closure of the Old Pier in the 1990s. Its final icon, mounted at the far end of the island, was the prototype for Concorde's nose which sat there pointing seawards.

Overlooking Birnbeck Island, though now thickly clad with sycamore trees, is the Iron Age hill-fort of Worlebury. It stretches from east to west with multiple ramparts of two

Seats on the side, looking south-eastwards to the Royal Pier Hotel (right)

Promenade view, from Anchor Head, to Birnbeck Island with foreshore enlarged by low tide

banks and five ditches defending the eastern entrances. Inturned entrances, 13 feet wide, can be traced in the north-east and north-west corners. Two lesser banks lie further east as contemporary outworks. A massive bank defends the vulnerable south side, protecting more than 10 acres, but the precipitous slope was adequate for the northern edge above Sand Bay.

Excavation in Victorian times showed the ramparts were constructed around triple internal walls of carefully laid stone. Though there is now strewn stone everywhere the core building work had been done with great skill. Grain storage pits were found across the interior, cut 6 feet deep into solid rock, which had been filled with rubbish at the end of their useful lives. There also seems to have been a Romano-Celtic shrine which yielded a Doulting stone carving of an earth goddess standing in an arch of foliage. Either in Iron Age times, or during the Roman conquest, the hilltop had been stormed, as some 100 skeletons showed signs of violent death.

THE WALK

For a strenuous 6-mile exploration of these wooded hills, park and start near the Royal Pier Hotel (ST 309 623). Set off northwards along Kewstoke Road, with Birnbeck Island down to the left and the villas of the Technical College up to the right. In 300 yards you enter a toll road and then turn right, up into Weston Woods on Worlebury Hill. You are now heading eastwards. Take the path along the northern slopes, straight ahead to the communications mast and water tower in 1500 yards. Keep them to your left and then turn left, on a path north-eastwards and downwards, to the right of another toll gate in 800 yards.

Here turn right, eastwards along Kewstoke Road, to St Paul's Church in 400 yards. In the Victorian rebuilding of the chancel a carved stone reliquary was discovered with a blood-stained wooden chalice, which was claimed as the blood of murdered Archbishop of Canterbury Thomas à Becket – from Woodspring Priory which had been dedicated to him – hidden after the Reformation. Turn right, up the steep flights of Monks' Steps – given to the National Trust in 1936 – which are also known as the Hermit's Steps and St Kew's Steps. Cross the road on Monks' Hill and turn left in Woodspring Avenue in 250 yards and then upwards again on returning to Monks' Hill in 75 yards. On the top, in another 200 yards, turn left along Worlebury Hill Road and follow it north-eastwards to the end of the golf course in 1200 yards.

Edwardian turnstiles at the end of the age of ferries

On reaching the Old Observatory – a converted tower windmill – turn right and then right again into walled paths along the southern slopes of Worlebury Hill. You are now overlooking Milton suburb and Weston town. Public paths weave around the hillside above the houses and bungalows of Hawthorn Heights, Hawthorn Close, Pleshey Close and Balmoral Way. Keep on the slope rather than taking either downward or upward options until you are in limestone grassland above the precipice of the old quarries in 1300 yards. Here ascend north-westwards, to the left of Ranscombe Farm, and follow its drive to Fairway Close in 200 yards.

Rejoin Worlebury Hill Road. This time turn left, westwards, and walk the length of the track into Weston Woods in 600 yards. Pass to the left of the reservoir in 900 yards and continue westwards along the top to the path junction in 400 yards. Again, stay on the summit, beside the site of Picwinnard Cairn, and reach the stony outer defences of Worlebury in 700 yards. Proceed for the length of the hill-fort and then descend the steps to Camp Road and the Retreat in another 700 yards. From here return to Kewstoke Road and the municipal gardens above the Royal Pier Hotel.

New church in suburbia, seen from the old church, at Uphill

10

WESTON-SUPER-MARE AND UPHILL

Ancient hills frame the south side of the wide valley at Weston-super-Mare. The ruins of the parish church at Uphill and a tower windmill overlook the Axe estuary. Here, beside the creek to the south of the present boatyard, ingots of Roman lead from the mines around Charterhouse on the Mendip Hills were exported from a port at the end of one of the busiest industrial roads in the West Country. Rough pasture above, now an informal open space and nature reserve, is known as Walborough, with the name having been used in Saxon times for a Bronze Age round barrow which was used as a boundary marker. There must have been a Roman signal station and the logical place for it is on the site of the church. A nearby mound marks the site of a medieval beacon.

Uphill's ancient church is half open to the sky

Between the outer churchyard wall and a precipitous quarried cliff there is a triangle of rough grass with the rusting stakes of Second World War anti-invasion defences. There has been a windmill here since the thirteenth century with the present circular building having become derelict by 1829 and later converted into an observatory. The Observer Corps monitored Luftwaffe bombers from it in 1940. The former mill is now a beacon, having been topped in 1988 by a replica Armada-period fire bucket.

Old St Nicholas Church is full of blocked and locked doorways. It had a priest's door in the south wall of the chancel, Norman arches on each side of the nave, and now has iron bars across the 1904-dated porch. By Edwardian times the strongly buttressed tower and now roofless nave and chancel were relegated to the status of a mortuary chapel. Its companion, the replacement St Nicholas Parish Church down among the flat streets of Victorian suburbia, was built in 1844 and extended in 1892. The list of rectors starts with the earliest recorded pre-Reformation priest, John de Gidding, in 1318. Weston-super-Mare, the upstart town to the north, encroached throughout the nineteenth century, bringing with it a retirement zone shadowed by the Royal West of England Sanatorium.

A tower windmill is Uphill's other exposed landmark

Uphill Manor, a castellated house, was the seat of the Knyfton family. Its entrance lodge fronted parkland grounds of 36 acres. Reginald Benett Graves-Knyfton was the lord of the manor at the turn of the twentieth century. There was then a Bleadon and Upton Station (stationmaster Robert Payne) on the south side of Upton Junction where the

Great Western Railway bypasses the Weston loop and continues straight on to Worle Junction. Village facilities survive along Uphill Way, north of Old Church Road, with traditional nautical names for the Dolphin Inn and the Ship Inn.

Before expanding into Weston-super-Mare, the seaside village of Weston as it was at the turn of the nineteenth century had just a couple of dozen homes, almost all occupied by fishermen. In 1812 there were 160 inhabitants and one public house. The Parish Church of St John the Baptist was rebuilt in 1824 and provided with a new chancel in 1837. Several other churches followed. By 1891 there were 2801 houses and 15,864 residents. The Edwardian population broke through the 20,000 barrier to make it the second largest town in Somerset. Only Bath was bigger, though it had dropped from its Georgian peak of 60,000 to a slightly less crowded 52,000. Weston now has 65,000 residents. Both towns came into being as spas, with Weston offering sea air at a mean temperature 10 °Fahrenheit warmer than London, and an 'invigorating' dose of iodine.

The sea front was constructed in its present form in 1887, as a broad promenade of 2½ miles, with numerous shelters, seats and flights of steps down to the beach. Construction was by civil engineer T.J. Scoones from Bristol. The Manor House of the Smyth-Pigott

Boatyard and the creek (top) *at Uphill*

Weston sea front from the Old Pier to the Grand Pier (right)

family at the north end of the High Street became publicly-owned Grove Park. A rocky outcrop between the sands and Anchor Head was bought by the local authority in 1896 and turned into Knightstone Causeway, with swimming baths and a theatre, plus a Marine Lake added later on the north side. The first section of the Grand Pier, opened in 1904 at the end of Regent Street, is now all that survives – too short for maritime use – of a design that was intended to be 6600 feet in length.

THE WALK

The more characterful sides of Uphill and Weston can be combined in a 3-mile mixture of town trail and seaside stroll. Park and start from the lay-by near the Dolphin Inn in Uphill Way (ST 316 584). Set off eastwards, passing the Dolphin and the Ship, following Uphill Way to its junction with Uphill Road beside former Uphill Farm in 500 yards.

Turn left, north-westwards, along Uphill Road. Continue straight ahead into the path at the corner, at the back of St Nicholas Road and the Paddocks, and pass to the left of the tower of the Victorian parish church in 150 yards. Proceed for a further 100 yards to rejoin Uphill Road and continue along it for 300 yards. Uphill Manor is across to your right.

Brean Down (top left) *and Uphill boatyard and church*

Turn left opposite Windwhistle Road, westwards, into a public path between the Plantation and the playing-field which crosses the golf course in 500 yards. Turn left on reaching the foreshore behind the sea-buckthorn scrub. Follow it southwards to Slimeridge Farm, Black Rock and the Axe estuary in 800 yards. Brean Down is across the water. Beware that even when the tide is out there is no way across apart from a summertime ferry.

Bear left and follow the causeway southwards and then northwards, around the peninsula to return to Links Road. Then turn right. In 50 yards turn right again and follow the right-hand path through the boatyard. This returns you to the causeway beside the creek and brings you to barrow-topped Walborough in 800 yards. Bear left, up and over ancient Uphill, via its windmill and old parish church, to descend to the Dolphin and the Ship in another 800 yards.

Steep Holm visitors surge ashore, up the beach, below dramatic Tower Rock outcrop

11

STEEP HOLM AND THE BRISTOL CHANNEL

First impressions last. Strangely, on first writing about Steep Holm I imagined a grassy Scottish-style rock, which was about as far wrong as it was possible to be, but the erroneous original mind picture still returns. Many of its visitors from Weston-super-Mare also have a shock on finding that their offshore island – the final outcrop of the Mendip Hills three miles off Brean Down – not only has a full-sized sycamore wood but is smothered by impenetrable vegetation including a rampant lush Mediterranean pot-herb, shoulder high, called Alexanders. If it is a clear day they are treated to breathtaking views of the entire Bristol Channel, from Foreland Point at Lynmouth and the waters off Lundy, upstream to the Severn Bridge and Berkeley power station.

Loaf-shaped profile of Steep Holm as seen from the eastern approach

The second memory is getting there. Weather and tides often make it a mission impossible. That was the verdict – 'insurmountable access difficulties' – by John Cripwell of the National Trust who rejected an offer of the island from the Wharton family's Halswell Estate. As a result they contacted me instead, to ask if it could be considered for the nature reserve monument for the broadcaster Kenneth Allsop. He was a close friend and I had been trying to buy his favourite hill in Dorset. Steep Holm had us looking at a different channel. My first visit, with author John Fowles and television producer John Percival, took place in December 1973 and was deceptively easy. The flat sea, on a day as grey as Mendip stone, was not the norm for the Bristol Channel at any time of year. A combination of south-westerly winds and tidal surges that are the second strongest in the world can make getting there and attempting to leave like a re-run of conditions endured in the Battle of the Atlantic.

My third discovery was that wartime analogies were not inappropriate. The island had been violated and abandoned with only a cursory clear-up when the Royal Artillery had stood down its Fixed Defences Severn. The Army had occupied Steep Holm from July 1941 until April 1945 when 570 Regiment and its 6-inch anti-ship guns were with-drawn. The brick and rusting corrugated iron, and smashed tortoise stoves, of dozens of Nissen huts were everywhere, projecting from the bushes and causing the perimeter path to divert around obstacles or otherwise climb across mounds of rubble. It had the appearance of the archetypal bomb-site.

Helicopter rescue for a Steep Holm visitor injured on the cliffs

Worthwhile history had also been left lying around. There were eight 7-ton rifled muzzle-loaded cannon from the 1867-dated Palmerston Follies which had put the first gun emplacements across the Severn estuary. Indeed it was the only Victorian heavy gun battery still complete with its weapons; then eight out of ten of them. Now there are nine, as I found another with a metal detector, lying beneath the concrete floor of the Second World War battery observation post at Rudder Rock.

I was hooked and wardened Steep Holm for the next quarter of a century, clearing wartime dereliction and rebuilding its inn, which had been demolished by explosives when the Royal Engineers fortified the island in 1941. The work of hundreds of volunteers has restored a magical place that performs for human visitors as well as wildlife rarities that make it unique. My role has passed to Chris Maslen and his partner, Jenny Smith, and the Kenneth Allsop Memorial Trust is now chaired by retired Crewkerne veterinary surgeon Tony Parsons.

As its huge coastal gullery declined with avian botulism, caused by the introduction of plastic bin liners which generate optimum conditions for anaerobic *Clostridium* bacteria in hot weather, other species did better. The cormorant cliffs are the busiest in the Bristol Channel. Peregrine falcons returned to breed and a dependable supply of racing pigeons is a major element in their diet.

Steep Holm has the only cormorant cliffs in the Bristol Channel

Muntjac deer, introduced by the author in 1978, found niche conditions not that different from their native island homes in south-east Asia. Slow-worms are as long as any in Britain, sometimes with bands of electric-blue markings, but finding record specimens is difficult as most have had their tails plucked by the gulls. Myxomatosis, maliciously brought to the island before our time, put paid to a distinctive reddish-coloured colony of rabbits which dated back to medieval warreners, and the Black Monks of the island's Augustinian Priory of St Michael.

The plant life is spectacular. The purple-petal wild peony, of single rather than the clustered blooms familiar in gardens, produces autumn heads of black (fertile) and red (infertile) seeds. These were used in herbal medicine and the plant must have been taken to the island by the monks, who also brought the wild leeks from which the eighteenth-century naturalist Linnaeus would receive his lectotype of the species. The garlic-tasting bulbs have the chromosomes $2n=48$ and are the plant's only method of sustaining itself as the impressive flower-heads do not set viable seed. Caper spurge, an almost architectural succulent milk-weed, and henbane are other nature-reserve rarities from the monastic medieval pharmacopoeia.

Sadly, the island has lost its greatest benefactor, Baroness Wharton, who was known to all as Ziki and acted as spokesman for the RSPB in the House of Lords. She died in the spring of 2000. In 1976 she honoured her late mother's wish that the island should be saved for conservation. The island was already being cared for and managed under a licence, and Ziki insisted that the freehold purchase price should be 'the amount you have left in the fund'.

It was embarrassing to admit that this had fallen to £7500 and was insufficient, in John Percival's words, 'to buy a semi-detached house in Ealing'. John Fowles personally ensured it was rounded up to a slightly more credible £10,000 and so the purchase was completed. Sale was the wrong word for it. Effectively the island was Ziki's gift.

Access is by pre-booked boat trips from Knightstone Causeway at Weston-super-Mare. Optimum landing times are either ninety minutes before high tide or ninety minutes after the tide has turned. The boat usually takes between forty minutes and an hour to reach the island which is a little more than 5 miles offshore. Though it is only a 2-mile walk, to do a complete circuit and interior crossing of Steep Holm the terrain is demanding and there is so much to see that it will take a couple of hours at least. You will have plenty of time as the return to Weston-super-Mare will be with the evening tide.

THE WALK

Approach Knightstone Causeway along either Knightstone Road or Birnbeck Road and turn seawards beside the Marine Lake. Park and start from Knightstone Causeway (ST 312 618). Set off on your island exploration from the main landing beach. In the summer of 914 Viking raiders drew their longboats up the pebbles and occupied Steep Holm. Climb the steps to the Second World War quay and boathouse.

Next up the path, beside the stone wall in 50 yards, is John Baker's Inn of 1832. It was blown up by the Royal Engineers when they fortified the island in 1941. Since 1980 it has been slowly undergoing reconstruction as a wardening depot. On a clear day you can see upstream to the supports of both Severn Bridges. Attached to the inn is the 16-line wartime telephone exchange, in a concrete box, which was served by underwater cables.

In a further 50 yards you come to a corner. Go straight on and pass to the right of a railway winch-house in 10 yards. Then in 7 yards you pass to the right of a second wartime building. Continue just a few feet to its next corner. From here, to the right, a set of 18 steps descend to the steel capping of 1941 that covers the Monks' Well. Perhaps it is older than that, and Roman in origin, as it provides the only natural water source on

Island birdman and Allsop Trust chairman Tony Parsons

Island ferryman Martin Woolls en route from Weston-super-Mare

Cliffside clump of the island's famous flower – the wild peony

the island. From it you have a good view of the sister island of Flat Holm, the southern-most point in Wales, and its lighthouse.

Retrace your steps to the main path and continue uphill. Pass the ruin of Cliff Cottage. Otherwise known as Smugglers' Cottage this has the island's rock-face as its back wall. Inset is a slate plaque:

This island of Steep Holm was bought by public subscription in the year 1976 to preserve the memory of the writer and broadcaster Kenneth Allsop, 1920–1973.

Carry on uphill. The rails through the sycamore trees are a military incline railway. Laid in 1941 it is actually the 60-centimetre gauge track of a German field railway that was captured on the Western Front in the First World War. It was then put in store and brought here for use against its makers in the next war. Steep Holm bristled with guns to protect the ships that had survived the U-boats in the Atlantic but then had to anchor in the Bristol Channel to wait their turn to be unloaded at Barry, Cardiff, Newport and Avonmouth.

Turn right at the next corner, in 150 yards. Then turn left, in 30 yards, up a flight of steps. Go straight ahead at the top and then explore Garden Battery war-works to the left of the path. There is an explanatory memorial:

The island's four Second World War 6-inch gun batteries were built by 930 Port Construction and Repair Company of the Royal Engineers and the Pioneer Corps, for the Royal Artillery in the defence of freedom, July to October 1941. This stone is a memorial to all who served on Steep Holm and in the Fixed Defences (Severn). It was unveiled on the occasion of the fiftieth anniversary of the island's fortification.

Beside it is a 7-ton, 7-inch bore, Victorian cannon. This rifled gun barrel from the last generation of muzzle-loaders was made at Woolwich Arsenal. You will come across eight more as you walk around. Up to the right is the 1868-built remains of its original stone barbette, with an earlier Georgian cannon sticking up from the ground as the pivot for its carriage. This was hauled around a circular rail. Above is a Second World War gunnery range-sighting instrument pillar, itself carrying a later memorial: 'Remembering Harry Cox, custodian of the birds and flowers of Steep Holm, 1930–1949'.

Follow the main path along the southern side of the island. In 50 yards you pass another concrete 6-inch gun battery, looking out across Bridgwater Bay, and then a wartime

Waverley paddle-steamer moored below Tower Rock

generator house, which powered two searchlight posts on the cliffs, 200 feet below. Next, in 50 yards, you come to a path which drops away to the left. An optional diversion, if it is safe enough to use, it descends across a scree slope to South Landing. This is a picturesque spot with a searchlight post, Victorian limekiln, and the remains of a wartime stone jetty. Offshore is Calf Rock.

Proceed along the top path and pass a railway winch tucked into the privet scrub at the top of the South Landing incline. You will reach the island's Palmerstonian period barracks block in 150 yards. Its partner and the grand strategy is discussed in the entry for Brean Down. There is a key-stone for Queen Victoria and a lamp bracket above: '1867 V.R.' The building was reused as the Second World War NAAFI and the counter, which now serves as the island's café, is on a wall which supported a stage for visiting ENSA concert parties. Now the building functions as a souvenir shop and is bunked out with emergency accommodation for stranded visitors. Outside there is a Georgian 24-pounder cannon dated around 1800, displaced from Summit Battery during the Second World War and brought here as a display piece, in a helicopter-lift in 1986.

The path continues westwards, beside the toilets and a marker stone. Incised 'W.D. No. 22', this shows one of the corners of a parcel of ground leased by the War Department in 1865. It carries the Government's broad arrow and is one of 28 such stones that delineate each plot that was acquired when there were fears that Britain would be sucked into the turmoil of the Franco-Prussian War. These are dubbed Palmerston Follies – Viscount Palmerston was the Prime Minister – but they served their purpose in that they never had to fire a shot in anger.

Rebuilt inn arising between the beach and a sycamore wood

Explosives expert John Pitfield (right) fires a Georgian display-piece beside the barracks

Next along the path, in just 10 yards, you turn right and climb five steps to the island's principal peony clump. This Mediterranean plant flowers pink in early May and has dramatic pods of black and red seeds in September. Steep Holm has long been famous as its British location, where it has naturalised into the wild, and it was immortalised in a romantic poem by William Lisle Bowles.

Return to the perimeter path, beside clumps of wild leek, where the next botanical rarities are henbane and caper spurge. The latter, architecturally-shaped, is a succulent. Both were herbal introductions: likewise the Alexanders – in the plural it has lost its apostrophe for Alexander's herb – which escaped from captivity in the monastic garden. It is the island's commonest plant and was grown as a herb for the pot, its stem being blanched like celery. Now it is everywhere, thriving in the mild coastal air as a lush yellowish-green version of cow parsley, in the first half of the year. Dry stalks, 5 feet high, are loaded with seed from July onwards. Next along the path, to the left, is a wartime incinerator.

In 175 yards you come to Split Rock Battery, a scheduled ancient monument, with 1868-built Victorian fortifications complete with their two cannon and underground shell and cartridge stores. These are accessible, down two flights of steps, and on top is a Second World War concrete base – with a circle of 12 nuts – on which one of the island's six 40-mm Bofors anti-aircraft guns was positioned.

Rudder Rock opens at low tide, at the island's western tip, beneath a wartime searchlight post

Onwards, in 200 yards, you come to the western tip of the island above the rock-arches of Rudder Rock. The next land due west is Goose Cove, Newfoundland, in some 3000 miles. The archaeology around Rudder Rock is particularly complicated. The mound to your right, above two Victorian magazines, was enlarged in 1866 from a 'beacon barrow' that was probably a Roman signal station. It kept watch for Irish raiders and passed semaphore messages to the fleet based at Cardiff Castle. On entering the 1941-built battery observation post you'll see that it is literally built on top of a Victorian cannon. The author discovered this with a metal detector, in 1981, and broke through the floor to prove the point.

Seawards are the remains of a steel gun emplacement that was blown apart by the cruiser HMS *Arrogant* in 1898. The attack was to evaluate the merits of the new steel armour compared with conventional stone and concrete defences. Next towards the open sea and the main shipping lane of the Bristol Channel is a flight of 76 steps down to a breathtaking viewpoint overlooking a 1941-built searchlight post.

Your next objective is the other way, eastwards and upwards, at Summit Battery in 150 yards. Here a pair of Victorian gun batteries are topped by twin 6-inch gun emplacements of 1941. The two Victorian cannon survive, with the second displaced to the pathside. It displays Queen Victoria's cipher with the motto of the Order of the Garter: *Honi soit qui mal y pense* (Evil on him who thinks evil of it).

Upwards and seawards is the island's hyperactive sky. Aerial activity features the impressive great black-backed gull, lesser black-backed gull, herring gull and cormorant. All nest on the ledges below. So too, in some years, does the peregrine falcon; you may also see jackdaws and ravens. Next along the path, in 25 yards, is a wartime generator house, then in 80 yards, a flight of steps facing Flat Holm and the coast of South Wales. Affectionately known as 208 Steps (after the 208 medium-band frequency of independent Radio Luxembourg) they descend to a searchlight post which doubles as a bird hide. The spot is totally exposed to elements and runs through the air like a ladder propped against the cliff: no place to be in crosswinds or if the concrete has a slime of guano.

Back on firm ground, in 125 yards, you come to the concrete bases of wartime Nissen huts. Named for British engineer Peter Norman Nissen, these structures of rounded corrugated iron housed the island's 200 wartime gunners. After the seventh hut site you are at Laboratory Battery. This Palmerstonian fortification is largely intact, with underground magazines, and two cannon.

You are now back in the scrub-zone of bramble and privet. Listen and look for the elusive Muntjac deer. The next gun battery, in 100 yards, is Tombstone Battery (named for the monastic memorial stone found here and now displayed in the barracks). It is a single barbette with one cannon. Around 15 yards after this gun barrel the path forks and you turn right. In 60 yards you come to the ruins of the farmhouse which was built in 1865. Enter it across the north wall and leave though the doorway, southwards. In 8 yards the path bends to the left through the bushes, to a tenement built in 1776 for stranded seamen or, more likely, freebooting smugglers.

The next ruin, the footings of a large L-shaped building, is the medieval Priory of St Michael. Built towards the end of the twelfth century it housed several 'regular canons' of the order of St Augustine. The altar end is at the east, now grassed, which faces Weston Bay. Rabbit warreners later occupied the building. It is the most sheltered and peaceful spot on the island.

Beside it, and the foundations of a wartime Nissen hut, grow wild peonies and the wild leek. A few steps bring you back to the main perimeter path. Turn right for a drink at the barracks or left if you are heading back to the boat.

The herring gull is the island's ubiquitous bird

Excavation of the priory ruins

Brean Down Farm (right) *and the Axe estuary* (centre)

12

BREAN DOWN AND THE AXE

At high tide the island-like peninsula of Brean Down juts out 2 miles into the turbid waters of the Bristol Channel. Hours later, seen from the great expanses of sand to the south or the mud-flats to the north, its status is reduced to being just another headland. This green hog's back of carboniferous limestone is the mainland seaward extremity of the Mendip Hills. In 1974 it became the north-western corner of the reconstituted county of Somerset.

It was then the favourite contender for the English landfall of a proposed tidal energy barrage across the Bristol Channel, from Lavernock Point, near Penarth. Lines on the futuristic map put it coming ashore at Fred Pontin's caravan camp between Brean Farm and Brean Down. The environmental downside to the scheme was its coupling with plans for a motorway as a bolt-on extra to defray some of the enormous construction costs. This was to have left the M5 in the shadow of Brent Knoll, across the wetlands, and linked Somerset with South Wales.

Brean Cove and the southern cliffs with Steep Holm beyond (centre)

By the end of the century, upstaged by wind farms in the North Sea, the plans were on hold. Privatisation of the energy industry and European protection for the mud-flats, to safeguard their wading birds under the requirements of the Ramsar Convention, had amounted to insuperable hurdles. For the foreseeable future the 320-feet summit of Brean Down will remain in splendid isolation separating Weston Bay from Bridgwater Bay. The 160-acre peninsula was given to the National Trust by the old Axbridge Rural District Council to commemorate the Festival of Britain in 1951.

The promontory is a Site of Special Scientific Interest and its botanical speciality is the rare white rock rose. Growing on the south-facing escarpment, where it is locally prolific, it is at the northern limit of its world range. Much less conspicuous, also very uncommon, are Somerset hair grass and dwarf sedge. Goldilocks is another botanical rarity.

You are more likely to spot a variety of birds. There is a good chance of glimpsing peregrine falcons and ravens. Certainly you will see gulls and cormorants en route to and from their offshore refuge on Steep Holm. Landward, depending on the time of the year

Seaward view of the Brean Down peninsula

and whether or not the tide is out, there are liable to be flocks of ducks and geese and drifts of oystercatchers, curlews and dunlin working the mud-flats. Scrub and grassland birds include the meadow pipit, skylark and wheatear. Butterflies are notably the chalkhill blue and grayling.

History ripples across the contours of the whole headland. From beneath the ground there was the discovery of a layer of bones from prehistoric beasts. Tundra creatures of the Ice Age included mammoth, bison, reindeer, elk, arctic fox, lemming and wolf. Next came a crop of strongly patinated flint implements, notably arrowheads and knives, showing that man the hunter lived on Brean from Mesolithic through to Neolithic times. Then he began farming and changing the shape of the landscape. There are a number of Beaker-period round barrows which covered the Bronze Age dead. Earthworks at the centre of the down, since reused for Second World War defences, are from an Iron Age promontory fort.

Nearby is the platform of a Romano-Celtic temple, associated with the Mendip lead trade which had a port in the estuary of the River Axe, that was dated to between AD340 and 370 by an excavation in 1965. It may then have housed a hermit.

Pillow-mounds are artificial rabbit warrens. These earth and stone rabbit hutches were created by warreners who cosseted the valuable creatures, newly imported from France, until a hardier strain not only became acclimatised but at some point escaped into the

Hercules and shadow heading toward Brent Knoll

wider countryside. Brean is known to have been warrened in 1361 and provided coneys, as they were called, for coronation banquets.

Brean Down was chosen for a grandiose Victorian scheme to make it the national terminal for the West Indian mail packets. Lady Eardley Wilmot laid the foundation stone for Brean Down Harbour at a great celebration on 5 November 1864. Nature soon thwarted the scheme by showing the impracticalities of the location, where gales combine with tidal surges. The stone pier, which was to have carried a railway running along the northern side of the down, was swept away in a storm on 9 December 1872.

What has lasted, dating from 1866 to 1870, is an extensive fort, part of the vast national war-works that was devised by Viscount Palmerston to protect British ports and anchorages from the ramifications of the Franco-Prussian War. In the event, it was a conflict that Britain avoided, which was what lead to these huge defences being dubbed Palmerston Follies. The secret joke was that the Viscount died while making love, on his billiard table, to a parlour maid. One wonders how that was explained to Queen Victoria.

The defences at the seaward end of Brean Down literally went out with a bang! Gunner Haines had been posted there from Steep Holm. He was unhappy at leaving his mates on the island and a week later, restless in the early hours of 6 July 1900, he took a carbine from above a comrade's bed. Haines walked from the barracks to No. 3 magazine and discharged the rifle down a ventilation shaft into 'pretty well three tons of powder'.

The resultant bang woke his former pals on the island. On Brean Down it left Haines dead, two 7-ton muzzle-loading cannon destroyed, and masonry littered over a radius of 200 yards. The inquest verdict: Temporary insanity.

Another sound from over these waters had already gone into history. The world's first radio transmission across the sea was beamed by Guglielmo Marconi from Brean Down to Lavernock Point in 1896. The distance was only 9 miles but Marconi realised the commercial potential of his achievement. By November that year he had established the Wireless Telegraph Company, at the Needles, Isle of Wight, as the world's first permanent wireless installation.

Second World War refortification of Brean Down, for coastal guns of the Royal Artillery in the Fixed Defences Severn, was accompanied by its use in experiments for the secret war. Out on the headland there is a rocket launcher, with two parallel rails, 60 feet long and 13 inches apart. They point into the Bristol Channel, to a spot just north of Steep

Detail of the rocket rails which are the earliest relics of their kind

Wartime searchlight post and the rail of an experimental rocket launcher

Palmerstonian fortifications facing Flat Holm and Wales

Holm, at an angle elevated 10 degrees from the horizontal. This was used to perfect the ship-launched anti-submarine missile Amuck.

Such is the diversity of the military, ancient and natural history that you stumble upon in the course of a 4-mile walk. You have the freedom to roam but keep clear of the unfenced cliffs. On a summer day in 1992, the author and a colleague spotted flares and watched a yellow RAF rescue helicopter winching up the body of a young man, as a lifeboat stood by offshore. He had fallen down the southern side, apparently having tried to cut the corner back from the fort to the car park, by taking the southern seaward slope. So, you have been warned – take care, and follow the directions.

THE WALK

Approach Brean by turning westwards off the A370 between Burnham-on-Sea and Weston-super-Mare and turn northwards along Warren Road, which is the coast road, to Brean Down. Park and start from the car parks beside Squires Gate and the Cove Shop (ST 297 586).

Set off towards the inland end of the great headland. The public path is along the track to the right of the Bird Garden and then bends to the right. Keep on this main farm road for half a mile to Brean Down Farm.

Here the track splits in three directions, but do not take any of these. Instead turn sharply left, beside a telegraph pole, about 25 yards from the garages. It is a narrow path, uphill through the bushes, above a slope smothered in ivy and cuckoo pint. Emerge through a fence onto the south-facing escarpment above the farm. Glance behind you for a view of the Axe estuary snaking through the mud-flats.

The path then crosses two stiles to bring you on to the summit at a bend in the road up from the aviaries of the Bird Farm. Continue straight ahead along the hilltop, with the Mendip Hills behind you, the Somerset Levels to the left, and Weston Bay and Weston-super-Mare to the right. Birnbeck Island, with its Victorian pier, juts out from the Worlebury headland at the far end of Weston seafront.

That is the way forward but if you wish you can turn around and walk 400 yards in the opposite direction, to the inland end of the headland, for a more intimate view of the Axe estuary, Black Rock, and Uphill church and boatyard. From here you have your best chance of seeing flocks of duck, geese and waders. Do not try going any further, however, as there is no safe way down.

On setting off the other way, from the corner, the main track gradually descends seawards and runs the entire length of the northern slope. You are heading towards a point in mid-Channel, between the Holms which are the islands of Steep Holm (left) and Flat Holm (with the lighthouse).

In a mile and a half, which can be a painful distance in a north-westerly gale, you come to the Palmerstonian Fort. Sprat Beach is below, to the right, as a reminder of what was the primary catch of these waters. On the other side of the dry moat and barracks you turn right to see the underground shell and cartridge stores – separated to minimise the danger of explosions – and a George III cannon upended in the ground as the pivot for a gun-carriage and a Victorian rifled muzzle-loaded cannon.

Further out towards the sea is another Victorian barbette and then the two steel rails of Britain's oldest accessible piece of missile-launching hardware. Finally, also from the Second World War and overlooking the shelving Howe Rock, is the remains of a 1941-built search-light post. Bear right after recrossing the bridge above the moat. Pass between two concrete-built 6-inch anti-ship gun emplacements of a Royal Artillery Coast Defence Battery. Continue uphill beside the command and observation posts which were operational from 1941 to 1944. A lookout was maintained for German E-boats towards Steep Holm and into Bridgwater Bay.

Ensure you keep to the Weston side of the cliffs. Climb on to a rounded hilltop with close-cropped turf and pass an Ordnance Survey triangulation pillar, set at the edge of a prehistoric cairn. Next are the humps and hollows of an Iron Age settlement.

Midway between this and the next summit, after crossing a fence, you come to a lesser rise. This is the site of the Roman temple. From the next hilltop, after a few steps, you head along the top ground towards the Mendip Hills.

As Brean Down Farm comes back into view you pass a Bronze Age round barrow. After this burial mound the path follows the Weston Bay side of the outcrops, keeping to the left of them. Then caravans and the car parks are conspicuous to your right and you have two choices for your route down. Either take the steep flight of steps, or continue 200 yards and rejoin the hilltop road. This then bends to the right and is the gentler descent to the Bird Farm and Cove Shop. Round off the walk with a closer look at Brean Sands but do not venture across the flats at the wrong point in the tidal cycle as the water comes in much faster than you can return to safety. The sea has also claimed its quota of motor car misadventurers.

Gun battery barbette looking northwards up-Channel

Battery Observation Post, built in 1941, faces the offshore Fixed Defences Severn

Triangulation pillar and the view of Weston Bay

Lower light, out on the sands (right) *with Steep Holm beyond* (left)

13

BURNHAM-ON-SEA AND THE BRUE

Seaside spas developed as Georgian society fanned out from Bath. The Clarence Hotel, where the Esplanade meets Regent Street at Burnham-on-Sea, was built in 1796. More than a century later, crowds still thronged around the bandstand on the sea front, which was provided to celebrate King Edward VII's coronation in 1902. By the time of the next king, George V in 1911, it was being replaced by the Pavilion. Burnham Pier has shrunk to non-nautical proportions but used to stretch 900 feet into the Parrett estuary. To the south, the River Brue has its confluence with the Parrett, at the end of South Parrett beyond Holimarine and the Yacht Club.

The first Burnham Lighthouse, known as the Little Round Tower, was built beside the churchyard by Revd David Davies in 1801.

The River Brue flowing through Highbridge

In an unusually suburban location for such a structure, the Bridgwater Bay Lighthouse – now known as Burnham High Lighthouse – was built for Trinity House, to a design by Joseph Nelson, in 1831. The tapering circular tower stands almost at sea level, immediately behind the dunes, and its light is at 91-feet altitude. Despite such a comparatively low height it can be seen for nearly 20 miles. Its partner, Burnham Low Lighthouse some 500 yards seawards, rises from the estuarine mud on a platform of piles. Though all three are now redundant, the three Burnham lighthouses survive as a reminder that this was a busy inshore channel. Until 1882, when a new boathouse was built at Birnbeck Island, Weston-super-Mare, the local lifeboat was based at Burnham.

Near the High Lighthouse, beside Berrow Road, Ellen's Cottages commemorate Ellen Saunders. This set of ten almshouses 'for poor women' was provided in her memory, in 1868, by widower John Saunders.

The town became a terminus on the expanding railway system. An offshoot of the Somerset and Dorset Railway, built in 1854, crossed the Great Western mainline at Highbridge Station – midway between Bridgwater and Weston-super-Mare – and reached the sea at what is now the big car park at the south end of the Esplanade. The Somerset and Dorset was jointly owned by the Midland Railway and London and South

Western Railway Company. Passengers from Manchester and Birmingham, on the Pines Express to Bournemouth, changed at Evercreech Junction.

Burnham's southern bungalows lie below sea level, and many were literally so on the evening of 13 December 1981, after sea defences were overwhelmed. It was the coldest December since 1890, causing the North Atlantic jet-stream to track further south than usual, pushing a deep and vigorous depression across southern England. This coincided with the high water of a spring tide which was funnelled up the Bristol Channel. Having been predicted at 6.10 metres at 20.14 hours at Hinkley Point, the actual high water reached 7.40 metres at 20.25. There was also a surging swell in the strong winds. So much water poured over the beach at Burnham that bungalows around Maple Drive were flooded to a depth of a couple of feet. Industrial buildings were inundated, from Hinkley Point Power Station to the Esso refinery at Avonmouth, and considerable numbers of livestock drowned. Coastal defences have since been enhanced with ramps, causeways and metal gates. These can be rolled into place across beachside access

Wartime pillbox beside Cobb's Leaze Rhyne at Pawlett

The tidal section of the Brue from Burnham to Highbridge

Burnham-on-Sea and the Brue estuary

Leaning tower of St Andrew's Parish Church, Burnham

roads in the event of another emergency. That has been done on a few occasions but so far there has been nothing comparable.

St Andrew's Parish Church at Burnham, beside the Esplanade, gives a novel twist to the Perpendicular style with a massive leaning tower. Its splendid altarpiece is by Inigo Jones. Having been removed from Westminster Abbey it was acquired by a former Burnham vicar, the Right Revd Dr Walker King, who was Bishop of Rochester from 1809 to 1827. Dr Walker King, who built Burnham Hall, presented it to his old parish.

North of Burnham, between sand dunes now subdued by impenetrable banks of sea blackthorn, St Mary's Parish Church at Berrow has some surprising survivals. The effigies of a medieval gentleman and his lady lie in the churchyard, beside the nave wall, and have eroded into ghosts. On the slope above is the base and shaft of a fourteenth-century cross. Its elaborate top, finely carved in Ham stone with figures on all four sides, was hidden to spare it from Puritan desecration and has since been found and displayed in the chancel.

St Mary's, Berrow, lies in scrub-covered sand dunes

Seaward end of the Huntspill River at sluices into the Parrett

The Ham stone top of Berrow's ancient churchyard cross

THE WALK

Burnham's maritime setting spreads out around you on a 4-mile circuit, in a virtual square, of the meadows between the River Brue and the Huntspill River. Approach Highbridge on the A38 and park and start in the vicinity of Huntspill Road (ST 320 472).

Set off westwards from the south side of Brue Bridge, along the embankment, across the river from Clyce Road. New Clyce Bridge, in 500 yards, has giant sluices to restrain the sea from inundating the Somerset Levels. In 1300 yards you pass marshland at the mouth of the Brue. From here the sea defences turn south-westwards and you follow them for a mile to the next set of sluices on the Huntspill River which makes a straight cut through the Levels.

Here bear left, south-eastwards, either across the meadows on a public path to West Huntspill parish church or, as an easier option, treat the access road to the sluices as a permissive path. It joins the road in 1100 yards on the north side of Sloway Bridge. Here turn left, northwards, and go round the corner. In 200 yards, on the left, there is a path across the field to the churchyard, in another 200 yards.

The lighthouse overlooks St Christopher's Way

St Peter's Church was rebuilt in 1880, after having burned down in December 1878, and the east window memorial to former rector Revd Noll Thomas Ellison is a replacement. It had been insured. The onward route is across the road, into the housing estate where you bear right and continue straight ahead into the meadows. Here turn left, northwards, into a series of paths that cross a succession of footbridges across meadows and at the back of gardens for a mile behind the main road at Huntspill and Alstone. In a mile, from behind Adams Close and the houses in Huntspill Road, you will be back at the starting point beside Brue Bridge.

The light (top left) faced Bridgwater Bay

Bowering's Feed Mill (left) *and the canal entering Bridgwater Dock*

14

BRIDGWATER AND THE PARRETT

ith its right arm outstretched, the statue of Admiral Blake pointedly dominates Cornhill, in the centre of Bridgwater. His finger reaches intrusively towards a first-floor window above Burton Menswear. D.W. Pomeroy's bronze is a century old, having been unveiled to mark Blake's 300th birthday and the arrival of 1900. It has already witnessed the coming and partial going of the age of the motor car, local liberation having been achieved by pedestrianisation in time for the millennium. Bridgwater and the Admiral would have been synonymous in the public mind at a time when the enormous rise and fall of the Bristol Channel tides, oustripped only by those of the Bay of Fundy in Canada, brought a regular procession of vessels up the muddy estuary of the River Parrett. Daniel Defoe punningly observed that the Parrett was so dirty that it looked as if the 'parrots' of the House of Commons had washed their consciences in it. It is ruffled by twice-daily tidal waves – known as the Bridgwater Bore – with 'Bore Times' being posted beside the Town Bridge. At its best, with so-called spring tides, it reaches 3 feet in height and approaches at 5 miles per hour.

With the simplest and most descriptive of English place-names, for a bridge over water (though originally the 'borough on the water'), the town and its fortunes continued to be determined by those tides into recent times. Almost unbelievably, in the year when the Admiral was welcomed back to Cornhill, 2057 vessels with a total displacement of 131,884 tons came into the port of Bridgwater. Furthermore, the nautical activity was growing and reached 3055 craft of 189,494 tonnage in 1904. Only a few were sand-dredgers, our familiar workhorses bringing 'Holm sand' for the construction industry, from off the islands of Steep and Flat Holm. Almost all were coasters – carrying what was called 'coastwise' trade – before air freight was even a concept, and canals and the railways still fed that greatest of natural highways, the sea. Oil seed for animal feeds came in bulk from the Black Sea and the Baltic. Arrivals in Bridgwater were from 'every corner of Europe and ports down the entirety of the east coast of the Americas, from Newfoundland to Argentina'.

For some deliveries the tidal river did not stop at Bridgwater. The Parrett was navigable by barge to Langport and extended to Taunton by canal. The Bridgwater and Taunton

Admiral Blake and friend advertising Burton Menswear

Coleridge Green is named for Nether Stowey's poet, Samuel Taylor Coleridge

The Parrett below the River Parrett Inn

Canal was constructed in 1827 and brought into the docks in 1841. A total of 86 vessels, of 5254 tons in all, were registered as belonging to the port under the Merchant Shipping Act of 1894, but the town's fishing boats had to drop their 'BR' registration letters when it was deemed that because of the configuration of the Bristol Channel they operated inside the 3-mile jurisdiction of United Kingdom territorial waters.

Imports to Bridgwater a century ago sound almost medieval. Slates, coal, timber, grain and hides are logical enough, and linseed follows suit, but esparto and valonia now require a dictionary. The former, a strong grass from Morocco and Spain, augmented the supply of local reed as the mainstay of Somerset basket-making, and valonia was also from the Mediterranean, being acorns of a Levantine oak. These were ground down for tanning chemicals. Even the native conker crop achieved national strategic importance during the First World War, being collected locally by schoolchildren and sent by rail to the Royal Naval Cordite Factory at Holton Heath, Dorset, for a vital supply of acetone which was used in making the propellant for shells.

These days we may ask why Admiral Blake is the icon of Bridgwater. Robert Blake was born in the town in August 1599 – in Blake Street – the eldest of 12 sons of merchant Humphrey Blake and heiress Sarah Williams. As Bridgwater's Member of Parliament, Robert Blake followed the front-line in the Civil War and became governor of Taunton, and was given command of the Commonwealth Navy after the execution of Charles I. Familiar with challenging western winds and tides, he proved adept at organising block-ades of French ports, survived an engagement against the Dutch, and wiped out the Spanish fleet off Santa Cruz, Tenerife. Despite his republican roots, Blake evidently met with Victorian ideals of 'chivalrous character' and 'unselfish patriotism'. Oddly, despite the honour of a statue and paintings in his home-town, no authentic contemporary portrait of Admiral Blake exists. Pomeroy and other sculptors and artists have given us their best guesses. School friends remembered him, unflatteringly, as 'a short, squat, ungainly figure'. He died on entering Plymouth Sound on 17 August 1657, and was buried in Westminster Abbey, but his body was removed to nearby St Margaret's churchyard when King Charles II was restored to the throne.

Bridgwater has long been known for prime products, a tradition continued by British Cellophane, and in 1900 the town embraced 'Bath brick'. Sold to Bath, rather than coming from there, these were made 'from a peculiar kind of slime deposited on the banks of the River Parrett, within two miles of the town'. The process was known as 'scouring'. Millions of bricks were manufactured each year, as well as vast quantities of tiles, pottery and drainpipes. At the time of writing, in the opposite corner of the county, the Bridgwater pottery stamp can be seen prominently on a window-sill in front of the author, but is less conspicuous on the roof.

All this industrial productivity sounds more like the output of a town in the Midlands or the North. Breweries and maltings; iron foundries and perambulator makers; oil cake and cotton cake animal feeds; cement and plaster of Paris; collars and shirts; and a workshop specialising in Windsor chairs. Bridgwater was a big town, of 15,209 people in 1901, with something of a temperance feel in that, appropriately for a Puritan, its most famous son was celebrated by the Admiral Blake Coffee Tavern, in Eastover. The Anchor, on West Quay, and the Mariners' Arms in Northgate Road sound much more appropriate. Having a North Pole Inn brought a suitably cosmopolitan touch of whimsy. For parochial reality there is also the River Parrett Inn on Salmon Parade.

These days, in a town of 31,990 residents, Blake is honoured in his own land by the Admiral Blake Museum in Blake Street and the Admiral Blake Fish Bar in St Mary Street. Sneer not at the latter, for there he often has a queue.

High sandstone walls flank the canal as it passes under West Street

Town Bridge and the Fountain Inn (left)

Bridgwater Castle, as it was, on a casting for the 1883-dated bridge

THE WALK

For an around-the-town 3-mile circuit of Bridgwater's waterways turn north from the A39 and park and start in the vicinity of Victoria Park (ST 293 375). Set off from Coleridge Green, north-eastwards, to Bowering's animal feed mill and Bridgwater Dock Marina in 200 yards. In another 200 yards you come to Russel Place Pool which is overlooked by the Harbourmaster's House. Beyond turn right on reaching the River Parrett in 100 yards. Opposite, in the reed beds, are the remants of timber wharves. Bird life includes duck and geese, sedge and reed warblers, and herring gulls. Below, across the mud, otters leave their tracks.

Turn right, southwards, along the riverside path to the double bridges in 250 yards. Turn left across 1871-dated Black Bridge which took the railway into the docks. Then cross the eastern end of 1988-dated Chandos Bridge which carries The Clink road. On the other side follow East Quay. Opposite, on West Quay, Lions' Building is named for its terracotta gate-guards, and the blocked arch of the Watergate – between Nos 11 and 12 – led to Bridgwater Castle, with the remnants of its walls being behind Business Link.

The 1935-built balustrade of Victoria Avenue Bridge

Canal moorings at Rose Cottage, below the Old Taunton Road

East Quay houses the Somerset Brick and Tile Museum in the former kiln and tile-drying shed of Barham Brothers' Brickyard. The present generation of quay walls were raised in height in 1983. Their period 'street furniture' includes steps, bollards, bases and stumps of cranes, and authentic railings recast in original Victorian moulds.

Turn right across 1883-dated Town Bridge, in 300 yards, towards the Fountain Inn. Here there is a diversion of 200 yards, straight ahead along Fore Street from the replica Pig Cross, to visit Admiral Blake in Cornhill. Your onward route is southwards from the west side of Town Bridge (replacing an earlier iron bridge, from 1795, and triple-arched medieval stone predecessor). Having turned into Binford Place, follow the riverside to the library in 100 yards. Here continue straight ahead into Blake Park and pass its memorial stone to Blake's birthplace and Edward VII's coronation in 150 yards. Note the double dates – June 1902 was when it was scheduled, but the king had to undergo emergency surgery for appendicitis, and 9 August 1902 was the actual day. As for the Admiral, Blake Street and his home is westwards, to your right.

Go through the subway beside Blake Bridge in another 50 yards. On the other side cross a triangle of grass and bear right, along the cycle track, to join Old Taunton Road in 150 yards. Turn left, passing the apartment blocks of La Ciotat House, to Somerset Navigators' Boat Club in Rose Cottage, beside the bridge in 400 yards.

Cross the bridge and then turn left. Follow the towpath of the Bridgwater and Taunton Canal. Keep the waterway to your right for the rest of the walk. It takes you on a big loop around the western side of the town. The next bridge carries Taunton Road in 100 yards. The following one is beside Brownes Pond in another 150 yards. The next stretch is opposite Safeway and the YMCA and takes you under Albert Street in a further 600 yards. Here the canal is set in a deep cutting between 20-feet-high walls of red sandstone.

West Street is next, in 150 yards, and the canal then curves beside the school to Wembdon Road in 350 yards. Victoria Road follows in 75 yards – crossing a 1931-built bridge – with the Maltshovel above you to the right. The canal then follows Lyndale Avenue as you return to Coleridge Green and the marina in 500 yards.

Dockyard crane and canal boats in Bridgwater Marina

Autumn shades reflected below Wembdon Road Bridge

Stert Point with Burnham-on-Sea and Brent Knoll across the estuary

15

STERT POINT AND BRIDGWATER BAY

Stert Island, beyond the hamlet of Steart – yes, they are spelt differently – is the ultimate seaward extremity of the Somerset Levels. Stert Point, between the Parrett estuary and Bridgwater Bay, is the last grass on which one can stand. Beyond that it is all wetland, nothing but reed and mud; thousands of acres of mud … twice a day there is more of the parish of Otterhampton under water than above it.

Wetlands extend along both banks of the Parrett

Otterhampton is also remarkable in that it is once more providing a home to the otters of its name. Their tracks can sometimes be seen, but not followed, in the soft, black ooze that emerges in the 42-feet exposure –in terms of height – after the second greatest rise and fall of the tides anywhere in the world, caused by the funnelling effect of the Bristol Channel in tandem with the prevailing south-westerly winds.

Inland, on the west bank of the Parrett, is Combwich. Beside the yacht refuge – deep-set mud at low water – is the 8-feet-high Combwich Buoy of oak timbers 4 inches thick, which was made in Carver's Boatyard at Bridgwater in 1860. Now standing upside down, with anchor-point at the top, it was given to the parish by Colin Wilkins in 1991. There used to be many like it in the Bristol Channel, with a light and bell fitted to the flat topside of each.

These wetlands on either side of the Steart peninsula were designated a National Nature Reserve by the Nature Conservancy (now English Nature) in 1954. They have since been elevated into the status of international importance under a European treaty, thanks mainly to the bird life they support. Because of the mud, and its billions of marine worms, crustaceans, and diminutive shellfish, there are thousands of wintering birds. Generally speaking, the colder it is, the more that come. They fly south from the Arctic and westwards from Russia, often via other British refuges such as Morecambe Bay and The Wash, which are vacated as the weather bites at the edges of middle England.

Combwich Buoy (upside down) *in retirement*

The quantities are staggering. Surveys have yielded counts such as these. Waders: 20,000 dunlin and 12,000 knot. Ducks: 11,000 teal and 10,000 widgeon. Others: 30,000 lapwing and 2000 oystercatchers; plus the occasional peregrine falcon coming across from

Hinkley Point seen from the coastal marsh at Catsford Common, Stolford

Detailed view from the tideline

Steep Holm or up from Exmoor to pick off a few waders; or a short-eared owl prowling nearby Wall Common for a vole dinner. Some, though only a tiny fraction, stay to breed.

This 10-mile walk takes you all round the Steart peninsula, plus the picturesque stretch of coast eastwards to Stolford, almost as far as Hinkley Point power station. It then takes in the historic villages of Stockland Bristol (once owned by the city) and Otterhampton. The sea defences westwards to Stolford and the power station were rebuilt in 1978.

In all there are three Anglican churches en route to service hardly a hundred households. Nineteenth-century clergyman Revd Dr John Jeffery was rector of Otterhampton for a record sixty-seven years until his death in 1871, and bequeathed a welfare charity for the poor of the parish. St Andrew's at Steart was a 'mission church' built in 1882 entirely at the expense of Revd Henry Arthur Daniel who was lord of the manor.

Stolford and Hinkley Point

The landscape is the closest that Somerset comes to the Fens, with similar great skies, though there is a notable difference – the distant hills. These rim Bridgwater Bay for virtually the whole 360 degrees, starting with the Welsh mountains to the north, giving way to the Mendip Hills in the east, the Quantock Hills to the south-west, then Exmoor.

THE WALK

It is a long but easy walk, with hills to admire but not to climb. Instead you have to be prepared for wet feet but ensure you stick to the designated route. Straying into the marshes is not to be recommended, owing to the deep oozes, plus a potential posse of irate ornithologists. If you can pick your day and time, it is best to arrive on the peninsula two hours before high tide, so that the birds are being pushed up the mud-flats towards you by the rising water.

The duck pond at Cox's Farm is the closest thing to inland water at Steart

Approach Steart by turning north from the A39 at the Cannington roundabout, west of Bridgwater, and then turn right in Cannington village. Turn right in 2 miles to head for Otterhampton and then turn right after this village, along the flat no-through-road along the Steart peninsula, into the cul-de-sac hamlet. Park and start from the Bridgwater Bay National Nature Reserve car park, which is a field on the left in the middle of Steart, between Quantock View Farm and Dowells Farm (SY 274 459).

Set off left along the road, following it north-eastwards past Dowells Farm and Collards Farm. Next is rustic Cox's Farm, fronted by a busy duck pond, followed by the stern straight lines of Manor Farm. Here the tar ceases and the road in unpaved for its final half-mile to the tip of the peninsula at Fenning Island and Stert Point.

Ahead of you is a prominent bird hide, functionally defying architectural convention, with Brent Knoll and the line of the Mendip Hills behind. Though almost at sea level this is where to enjoy the aforementioned panoramic views clockwise around the Parrett Estuary. To the north are Steep Holm, South Wales, Brean Down, and Stert Island. North-east are the River Parrett, Burnham-on-Sea, and Brent Knoll. Eastwards are the Mendip Hills, with a central gash at Cheddar Gorge and the television mast to the right. East also is West Huntspill, across the estuary, with the church tower. South are the Somerset Levels. South-west are the Quantock Hills. West is Hinkley Point nuclear power station and behind it Exmoor, including Dunkery Beacon and the wooded cliffs beyond Minehead, projecting at the National Trust headlands of Greenaleigh Point and Hurlstone Point. The structure in the water is for the filters of the cooling inlet for the power station.

Bird hide with its border-guard-style architecture on Stert Point with Brent Knoll behind

On Stert Point, towards Stert Island, there are three smaller hides, much closer to the mud and the birds, with a fourth overlooking a scrape. Having visited these hides you turn towards Hinkley Point, heading south-westwards down the Bristol Channel shoreline. A footpath follows a low ridge beside the reed beds and Stert Flats. After passing the farms of Steart go through a gate into Wall Common.

Sand dunes beside Bridgwater Bay, at Wall Common

Wartime relic beside Stert Flats

The Parrett (left) at Combwich Reach

Continue to follow the shore to the sand dunes and the remains of a Second World War pillbox, with a National Nature Reserve sign beside it. Beyond this, walk along a stretch of stony road, with a grassy causeway to your right, towards an ever-larger power station, looking increasingly gaunt, austere and Soviet, even. A mile after the pillbox you pass a lagoon on the inshore side of the coastal causeway. Then, in a further 300 yards, the farmland wall to your left changes direction towards the south-west. This is Catsford Common, with Stolford Farm beyond.

Turn left down towards this kink in the wall. Go through the field gate 40 yards to the left of it. This public footpath enters the farmland where you bear right to the left-hand of the two gates towards the corner of the first pasture. From here you head south to the left-hand of another two gates, keeping Whitewick Farm to your right.

Then comes another gate, followed by the field to the left of the farm. Bear left but ignore the orchard gate. There are then two further gates in the left-hand hedgerow. Go through the first of these. You are now heading south, with a hedgerow to your right. Continue straight ahead at the end, through the gates between the Dutch barn and an implement shed. Keep going south, through the next gate, towards the pylons. Aim for the sag-point between the closest pair. There used to be a bridge over the rhyne at this point but at the time of writing it has still to be replaced.

If this is still the case, turn right on to a second public path that heads north-west to Chalcott Farm. Go through the gates and then turn left, in the pasture south of the farmhouse. This is the closest alternative rhyne-crossing, which is to the right of the closest pylon. From the bridge bear left to resume your course towards the sag-point to the left of this pylon.

Go through the gate in the corner and pass under the cables. Walk up the slope to Woolstone Farm and skirt the right-hand side of the first buildings. Then enter its yard. We were told to exit along the grassy strip to the left of the farmhouse but the legal line of path is from Woolstone Lane on the other side of the building. Go through the gate and continue southwards, towards Stockland Bristol on the skyline, with medieval settlement traces etched in its slopes. There are wooden footbridges in line with the dense hedgerow, followed by an historic arched stone bridge, which is the oldest crossing point in the entirety of this long walk.

From here head up the slope, to the gate in the top corner, beside the shed and pine trees. Walk up to the steps of St Mary's churchyard and then turn immediately right, through the garden gate opposite. Pass to the left of the house and go through the gate. Then in 15 yards turn left, across a stile in the hedgerow, beneath the electricity pole. Cross this arable field diagonally, towards the church tower and house on the other side. Go through the gate in the kink of the hedgerow and continue south-eastwards, to a foot-bridge midway along the dense lower hedgerow of this second arable field. Then head south, up the slope, and skirt the walled garden to the right of the house. Turn left on the other side, through the field gate, and walk down the lane into Otterhampton.

Pass All Saints' Parish Church and turn left at the junction, towards Steart. Turn right at the next junction, after Rose Cottage, into Steart Drove (which you will have driven along earlier).

Then turn right in 200 yards, through the field gate, onto a footpath immediately after South Brook which follows the watercourse south-eastwards for a mile to Combwich Clyce, where it joins the River Parrett. Here turn left and follow the flood defences northwards, towards an estuary half a mile wide. In a mile, at North Clyce, the Parrett Trail continues straight ahead, into Bridgwater Bay National Nature Reserve. To your right are reed beds, followed by expanses of mud, which with low tide and a degree of luck will be incised with otter tracks.

In about 1500 yards the coastal path approaches a pair of gates. Bear left, down to the lower one, and cross the stile beside it. This point, incidentally, is about 750 yards beyond the path turn-off currently shown on maps; which simply does not exist on the ground. Your alternative track is an unpaved farm road, raised on a causeway, with wet ditches on either side.

It passes between the fields and returns you to Steart in what feels like a long mile. Across to the left are Church Farm and the clump of trees around brick-built St Andrew's Church, with the 1847-built Bethany Chapel behind Channel View bungalow to the right of it. The path emerges in the centre of the hamlet, on the lane, opposite Dowells Farm. Turn left and your car is on the right.

Mud, yachts and the spire of Combwich church (right of centre)

North Clyce where North Brook flows into the River Parrett

Lilstock pebbles and the seaboard eastwards to Hinkley Point

16

KILVE AND LILSTOCK

Kilve village has retreated from the coast, inland along Sea Lane, leaving the parish church and Kilve Chantry in the meadows. The chantry was founded in 1329 by Sir Simon Furneaux to house five priests who were endowed in perpetuity to pray for his soul in St Mary's Church. Comprising a refectory, dormitory, still-room and granary, in post-monastic times the chantry became a farmhouse. It was gutted by fire in the 1850s and itself remains a ruin, with the house having been rebuilt to the west, and also a tearoom facing the sea.

Fossils on Kilve beach date from 200 million years ago, in the mid-Jurassic period, and its beds of blue lias include some of Britain's earliest ammonite fossils. Known as Kilve Pill, its landing place dates from before 1559 and was last rebuilt in 1840 and 1887, when a limekiln was added at the landward end. An enterprising attempt at extracting oil from underlying layers of shale was undertaken in 1924 after wartime shortages put a premium on home-produced fuel. Dr Forbes-Leslie founded the Shaline Company. His brick-built oil-retort house, which survives beside the car park, was the first structure to be built for the conversion of shale to oil. The project began to yield viable quantities but failed during the economic depression.

Kilton, the next hamlet to the east, is also a mile inland. St Nicholas Church, which was completely rebuilt in 1862, stands on rising ground with a panoramic view across to Minehead. Towards the sea is the even smaller hamlet of Lilstock – just a couple of farms – with redundant St Andrew's Church in a peaceful churchyard. The rest of the medieval church was pulled down in 1881, leaving the chancel as a mortuary chapel. A porch and bell-cote were added. It was restored as a labour of love by retired rector Revd Rex Hancock in 1993. Lilstock had been merged with Kilton but, as the combined population of the parish of Kilton-with-Lilstock numbered only 93, in 1901 it was absorbed into the adjoining parish of Stringston.

The beach at Lilstock is now much less busy than Kilve Pill but it briefly had its moment. Sir John Acland built a boathouse and a high-water jetty beside the stream in 1820. It became a port for the estate after Sir Peregrine Acland succeeded his father in 1589-dated

Kilve's blue lias cliffs are home to the earliest ammonites

Kilton's view of the nuclear reactors, with the Mendip Hills beyond

The Range Quadrant Hut overlooks the target area for naval flyers

The ruined chantry at Kilve

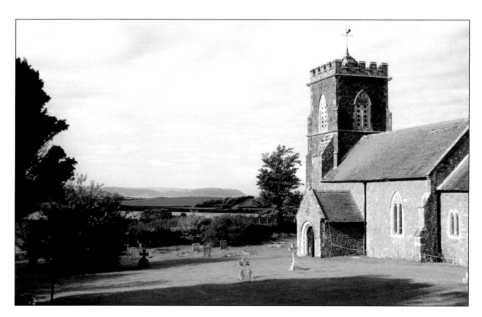

Kilton church and the skyline of North Hill above Minehead

Fairfield House near Stringston. Coal was imported from Wales. As well as supplying the estate this fired a limekiln on the cliffs. Pit-props were exported. In the middle of the nineteenth century there was a coastguard station and resident customs officer. The jetty was extended into a pier in 1860 and warehouses built at the landward end. Steamers called in a triangle of long-distance services between Ilfracombe, Burnham and Cardiff. By 1888 the Board of Admiralty was considering the possibility of a ship canal across the South West peninsula from Seaton on Lyme Bay to Lilstock on the Bristol Channel. All activity ground to a halt before the First World War and gale damage decided the matter by wrecking the pier.

THE WALK

A simple 6-mile coastal walk provides a circuit of Kilve, Lilstock and Kilton. Most of it is relatively level but there is one short climb. Park and start in Kilve (ST 149 430). Set off northwards along Sea Lane to Kilve Chantry and the sea at Kilve Pill in a mile. Here take the right-hand path up and over the knoll overlooking the stream and beach. You are heading eastwards, up-Channel, and pass the Range Quadrant Hut of Bridgwater Bay Bombing Range in a mile. Its aerial exclusion zone is controlled by Yeovilton Royal Naval Air Station.

Low cliffs to the east of the beach at Kilve

The ancient chancel at Lilstock

In another 1000 yards you come to the next scrubby stream that trickles across the beach. Turn right here, southwards beside a wood and cottages, along an untarred road to the lane in 600 yards. Then turn right, westwards through Lilstock hamlet, and pass the grassy entrance to St Andrew's Church on your left in 500 yards. On the opposite side there used to be a beer-house known as the Limpet Shell. From here you are heading south, uphill to St Nicholas Church in 900 yards. A path southwards from the far corner of the churchyard brings you back to the lane in 100 yards.

Turn right into Kilton, to West Kilton Farm in 350 yards, and a cottage 200 yards beyond it. Here, opposite the house, turn right into the pasture. Bear left into the corner of the field in 75 yards. Enter the big arable field and follow its left-hand hedgerow for 350 yards. In the next field you follow the track down into Lower Hill Farm in 250 yards.

Proceed straight ahead, uphill to the junction in 400 yards. Turn left for 100 yards in Hilltop Lane. Then turn right, southwards along Hilltop Lane, and follow a green lane south-westwards into Kilve in 600 yards. On reaching the main road, turn right along a footpath beside the stream, to cut the corner into Sea Lane in 150 yards.

Whitewashed tower on Kilve parish church

Blue Anchor eastwards to Gray Rock

17

BLUE ANCHOR AND QUANTOCK'S HEAD

Blue Anchor and Quantock's Head are the geophysical landmarks of this coast. The former, east of the 1921-built concrete sea defences and the Blue Anchor free-house, is called Gray Rock on the map but it is anchor-shaped towards the base and colour-contrasts with the adjacent red sandstone cliffs. Its banded beds of grey shale and harder blue lias rocks rise into another bulwark at Quantock's Head; together they provide the notable place-names hereabouts. Not that all these hamlets and villages are beside the sea.

St Etheldreda's Church at West Quantoxhead was rebuilt in 1856 with pink marble arcades. It stands on the north side of the A39 beside the drive to the Tudor mansion of St Audrie's House. The estate boasts many splendid ghost stories which include a horse and rider galloping along the A39 before vanishing into a wall, a horse-drawn fire engine seen on two occasions and a headless horse rider who emerges on New Year's Eve.

The end of the promenade below Blue Anchor free-house

High Victoriana also caught up with St Audrie's which was refronted in Gothic style by John Norton, in 1871, for Sir Alexander Bateman Periam Fuller-Acland-Hood. His son Alexander, who succeeded his father as 4th Baronet in 1892, was MP for West Somerset and Parliamentary Secretary at the Treasury. Created 1st Baron St Audries in 1911, he inherited a major collection of both Etruscan and Exmoor antiquities, plus the bones of a woolly mammoth found on the estate. Alexander Peregrine Acland-Hood, who succeeded his father as the 2nd Baron St Audries, lived at Fairfield House, near Stringston.

East Quantoxhead, almost 2 miles away, has another combination of church and mansion but on a much more modest scale. St Mary's Church is almost dwarfed by adjoining Court House, a manor of the Luttrells, from the thirteenth century. Captain Alexander Fownes Luttrell, son Geoffrey, and grandson Lieutenant-Colonel Geoffrey Walter Fownes Luttrell continued their occupancy through the twentieth century. Dunster Castle was their stately residence but this remains the family's private home.

Court House at East Quantoxhead faces seawards

THE WALK

Westwards, beneath Rydon Hill, Doniford is a main-road hamlet on the Swill, between holiday camps beside Helwell Bay, where the sea retreats for half a mile across mud and rocks at low tide. One has to admit almost total defeat in the attempt to find anything other than a 3-mile seaboard circuit as there is an almost complete absence of coastal rights of way. Park and start half a mile inland, in the field facing the millpond at the end of the road in East Quantoxhead (ST 137 436).

Set off north-westwards for 200 yards, to St Mary's Parish Church, which has an Easter sepulchre in the form of the alabaster table-tomb to Sir Hugh Luttrell (d.1521) and son and heir Sir Andrew Luttrell (d.1538). There is a fine fifteenth-century oak chancel screen and a 1633-dated Jacobean pulpit. In the porch the rector had a squint-window looking along the path from the great house so that he could prepare to welcome his benefactors and their dearly departed.

Now turn south-westwards, down across the grass to the field gate, beside the corner of the left-hand wood in 100 yards. You are heading inland towards West Hill. Cross the middle of the big field beyond to the lane in the far corner in 300 yards. Turn right, westwards, to the corner in 200 yards.

Finely-carved Jacobean pulpit at East Quantoxhead

Lias cliffs at Gray Rock with the shade and shape that gave Blue Anchor its name

Eastern view from Quantock's Head to Kilve, with the remains of a limekiln set in the cliff (right)

Victorian Gothic at St Audrie's Church with a West Quantoxhead resident

Proceed straight ahead, into a double-hedged green lane, and follow it westwards for 400 yards. Here, at the end of the second field on the right, turn right into sloping grassland with an ancient mound topping the rounded hill to the left. Follow the hedge northwards, keeping it to your right, and follow this permissive path to the sea beside David's Way in 750 yards. Here you join another permissive path and turn right, eastwards along the low cliff top fringed with scrub, with the shale geology spread out below in an almost artistic series of ridges.

In 900 yards you will pass Quantock's Head and turn right on reaching the stream to join a public path at the corner of the pasture in 50 yards. There is the ruin of a limekiln to the left and much less left of another set in the cliffs. Follow the grassy path southwards towards East Quantoxhead. In 700 yards it bends to the right, south-westwards, for the final 300 yards back into the village. Pass Old Mill House, still in operation by miller and baker Robert Wake into the twentieth century, and return to the church car park.

'Old St Audrie's Church' as depicted in 1836

Orchids nestle between the alabaster veins in Warren Bay

18

WATCHET AND WASHFORD

An industrial presence past and present is evident around Watchet. Paper and board manufacturers include the St Regis Paper Company in Wansbrough Paper Mill, C-Pack at Williton and the Two Rivers Paper Company at Pitt Mill, Roadwater. Watchet Harbour is tidal, comprising ten acres of mud at low water, and an entrance depth of 22 feet on a spring tide. When it was rebuilt by engineers James Arbernethy and Samuel Brown in 1861 it became the best of the small ports along this section of the Bristol Channel. Nature hit it hard with a gale in 1901 and 390 feet of the western breakwater was reconstructed in 1904. Steamers and coasters used a 560-feet pier to the north-east. As a reminder of how fickle weather forecasting used to be, Sir Alexander Hood donated a public barometer, which was the first application of science to an art previous based on hanging fronds of seaweed. The lifeboat station was established in 1875.

Returning mud to the sea at low tide during harbour reconstruction work

Other traditional industries included the iron foundry of J. Gliddon & Son, Stoate & Sons' flour mills, and a flourishing trade in cement, coal and malt. The notable late-Victorian export was iron ore from mines on the Brendon Hills, brought to West Quay by the West Somerset Mineral Railway which was built in 1858. From Watchet it was shipped to the furnaces and foundries of Ebbw Vale in South Wales – the land of Aneurin Bevan and Michael Foot – until production from the Somerset shafts was undermined by cheap imports from Spain.

Work on the broad-gauge West Somerset Railway began near Taunton in 1859 and it arrived at Watchet in 1862. The extension to Washford and Minehead, in 1874, completed a 25-mile line. The length from Watchet to Washford runs beside what is now the overgrown bank of the mineral line. The Minehead line was converted from Brunel's pioneering wide gauge to the ordinary and much more restrictive 4 feet 8.5 inches – which meant smaller and less stable carriages – on the weekend of 20 October 1892. Eventual incorporation into the Great Western Railway took place in 1921.

Cat-and-mouse game with the water to wash up at the end of the day

In the following century, caravans and camping provided the main trade along this seaboard, and literally saved the branch railway. It had failed to survive the chop under Dr Richard Beeching's axing of rural lines and closed on 4 January 1971. The track was due to be removed, and bridges broken, when Sir Billy Butlin and Somerset County Council intervened to underwrite the establishment of a new West Somerset Railway. They succeeded in reopening the line on 28 March 1976 and it has since brought back a succession of historic locomotives, some for period stays and others as guest visitors, to operate what is now Britain's longest steam line in regular seasonal service. Having faced 'every hazard known to railway preservationists' the project succeeded and validated the hopes of steam enthusiast Sir Gerald Nabarro MP. He visualised it becoming 'an example to all other privately owned lines' that would add 'a new and more grandiose aspect to the industry'.

Railwayana from less fortunate lines has found a new home at Washford Station which houses the Somerset and Dorset Railway Museum. Lines of rolling stock face signal boxes brought from elsewhere. One is from Burnham-on-Sea and has been fitted out in imitation of that at Midford. Beware of 'anoraks'. The author's visit was marred by one who insisted on collaring each successive visitor to tell us that the door is 'in the wrong place' and 'only the "Upper Inner Home" at plate 14 is from Midford'.

Signal levers from Wellow (left) *at rest in Washford*

British Railways class-4 locomotive working the bank above Washford

Paper remains the Watchet's prime product

Smart as paint railwayana: up-and-down tablet-control mechanism from Bath Junction

On the coast, around Cleeve Bay and Warren Bay, you are unlikely to find anyone coming between you and your imagination. Orchid-rich grassland drops down to the beach, across exposures of the 'celebrated alabaster rocks' in veins that used to be worked commercially. Mixed with gypsum, both being white, these beds contrast with those of blood-red conglomerate and light green limestone. Offshore are the traces of a submerged forest.

THE WALK

The railway and coast can be brought together in a 5-mile circuit from Washford. Park and start (or arrive by train) at Washford Station which is beside the A39 at the west end of the village (ST 044 412). Set off eastwards, beside the Washford Inn, and then turn instantly left, to walk the length of the left-hand wall, with house No. 62 to the right. After 50 yards turn sharp left and follow the footpath sign for the Old Mineral Line and Watchet. This path is sandwiched between the back gardens and the railway line. Turn left on reaching the road junction.

The outside of the harbour wall at Watchet, south-westwards towards the town

Medieval cross in Old Cleeve churchyard

Go under the railway bridge and then ascend the Monks Steps. These join Monks Path which is the narrow road up and over the hill to Old Cleeve in half a mile. On the hilltop you pass the stump of a medieval wayside cross. Having dropped down into Old Cleeve, turn right and follow the footpath sign for Blue Anchor which takes you through St Andrew's churchyard. Here there is a much more impressive preaching cross, plus the ancient parish chest in the porch, which is cobbled with beach pebbles.

Exit from the churchyard at the opposite corner to the one by which you entered. Here you descend the steps and then proceed straight ahead into an overgrown double-hedged trackway. In 200 yards this crosses a sunken section of ancient road with a flight of steps through the red earth on each side. Continue straight ahead, into the arable field, and bear left to cross it diagonally in a north-westerly direction. Cross the stile in 400 yards, near the corner, between the house and field gate.

Turn right on reaching the road and follow it uphill for 600 yards, into Cleeve Chapel then right again up a public footpath at the lower end of Huntingball Wood. This turns to pass to the right of the house and then continues up its drive. In 400 yards the top end of the path is a tarred road across Beeches Holiday Park to the B3191.

Make another right turn and then left after 30 yards, along a permissive path provided by Crown Forestry. This replaces a right of way which has been lost to coastal erosion. Walk through Three Acre Covert and Cridland's Copse as the track weaves through scrub and clumps of hart's-tongue fern to join the coastal footpath in 350 yards.

Go right, eastwards towards Watchet – but remember to turn around for one of the classic Somerset views towards Dunkery Beacon from the sea. Follow the cliff path for a mile, to beyond Crow Covert with its contorted ash tree, and Warren Farm. As you glimpse Watchet Harbour, protruding behind the headland, the path crosses a stile into a field and then turns left, into and across the next field. Head back into the woods where a diversionary path leads down to the beach.

Your route re-enters the scrub and emerges on a concrete road in 150 yards. Turn right, southwards up through Warren Bay caravan park, to the B3191 in 400 yards. Turn left along the main road, eastwards, for 150 yards. Just around the corner turn right through a field gate. This hillside incline, descending south-westwards, is signed to the 'Old Mineral Line'. You have a perfect view over the West Somerset Railway which emerges from beneath St Decuman's Church and Watchet Paper Mills into a long valley beside Kentsford Farm.

After 250 yards it is the moment to 'Stop, Look, Listen' – hopefully for a steam train – and cross the line. Turn right on the other side at the crossroads of paths. Follow the trackbed of the former mineral line. It passes Bye Farm and then follows the Washford River into Lower Washford in a mile. Turn right beside Old Cleeve First School and walk along the road to the railway bridge. Beside it, straight ahead, is the public path which returns you to Washford Station.

Steaming towards Minehead beside Kentsford Farm

Classic view of the High Street and Dunster Castle

19

DUNSTER CASTLE AND DUNSTER BEACH

Superlatives abound in and around Dunster. It is often called a village but is in fact the best small town in Somerset. The main street and Market Square has the 1589-built Yarn Market as its covered cross, with the older Butter Cross now in retirement on St George's Hill. George Luttrell built the Yarn Market and the family name abounds. The Luttrell Arms, originally the Dunster home of the Abbots of Cleeve, has fine stonework dating from 1500. By 1651 it was the premier local inn. The Nunnery in Church Street is a real rarity, being a fourteenth-century stone and half-timbered house, which overhangs the pavement. The Priory has almost disappeared but its dovecote can claim to be the most complete example in the world.

What makes Dunster so delightfully special is the way it nestles into a fold in a highly-gardened landscape. Peeking out of the trees above, on one side, is the embattled Folly Tower of the 1760s on Conygar Hill. Looming large, over the entire town, is the sandstone mass of Dunster Castle which was originally built by the de Mohun family. Elizabeth Luttrell bought them out in 1376 and the family remained in residence for precisely six centuries, until 1976 when Lieutenant-Colonel Sir Geoffrey Luttrell gave the castle and its grounds and gardens, including the eighteenth-century working Dunster Castle water-mill, to the National Trust.

Medieval stonework is everywhere, including the gatehouse of 1420, but the final form of the main buildings – and their parkland presentation – is due to Victorian architect Anthony Salvin. He retained treasures galore, including the 1681-dated dining room which is described by Sir Nikolaus Pevsner as having 'one of the most gorgeous plaster ceilings in South West England'. The keep used to be on the flat-topped summit of the tor but Salvin's touch of brilliance was to demolish the private chapel dating from 1722 – which he could still dismiss as 'new' – and replace it by the present 'mighty tower' which is now the distinctive shape of Dunster Castle.

The other Victorian touch is the sight and sound of steam trains running across the reclaimed land between the town and the present shoreline of the Bristol Channel. At Dunster Station the author was treated to the appearance of the current star performer

Lush leaves and palms giving an exotic touch to the Butler's Walk at Dunster Castle

Destination Minehead as named locomotive King Edward I *pulls out of Dunster Station*

on the West Somerset Railway. *King Edward I* is a Swindon-built 4-6-0 locomotive, made in 1930 and costing £7175. She steamed 1,570,015 miles before being condemned on 19 June 1962 and taken to Barry Dock scrapyard. Eventual rescue and renovation returned her to former glory and former Great Western Railway engine No. 6024, at 135 tons including the tender, is now the heaviest workhorse on the Minehead line.

THE WALK

A 5-mile circuit links the four major Dunster attractions of castle, town, station and beach. Approach Dunster along the A39 and follow National Trust signs into the Old Park, east of the main road traffic lights. Park and start from the National Trust car park below Dunster Castle (SS 994 437).

Set off from the entry kiosk, uphill into the inner grounds, for 100 yards. Then turn right and bear left in another 100 yards, up the slope beside the seventeenth-century stables, and under the thirteenth-century arched gatehouse in 75 yards. Turn right and climb the steps to the castle forecourt in 100 yards. Visit if you have the time.

Ancient walls were turned into a garden feature

Anthony Salvin's Victorian tower transformed the Dunster skyline

Dunster Beach, eastwards to Blue Ben, from the pebbles camouflaging a wartime pillbox

Dunster parish church from the Priory Gardens

On leaving from the main door, proceed along the drive beside the grass with the Tenants' Hall to the right. Then in 200 yards turn left into the bushes and climb the motte which was the site of the original timber fortress from Norman times to about 1200. Bear left in 50 yards to see the dogs' cemetery. Then climb to the top of the zigzag path in 200 yards.

Descend from the keep garden, beside the gazebo, to the Butler's Walk in 150 yards. Here, turn right and retrace your steps to the castle and gatehouse, returning to the stables in 400 yards. Turn left and walk down to West Street in 150 yards. Cross from Spears Cross Hotel to Chapel House art gallery.

Follow St George's Street up and around to Priory Lane in 150 yards. Turn right to see the parish church and then have a diversion along the lane, under the arch in 50 yards. The dovecote is on the left in 75 yards. It is unique in being complete with its 400-year-old timber potence which revolved to allow the monks to collect pigeon eggs. Opposite, to the right of the tithe barn, are the Memorial Garden and the walled Priory Gardens on the site of the Benedictine religious house.

Pigeon house potence (for nest collections) survives in the dovecote

The Luttrell Arms was the former home of the Abbots of Cleeve

On returning to St George's Street turn right beside the school and pass the thatched cottages and 1835-dated Vines Cottages at St George's Close. Proceed up St George's Hill to the medieval Butter Cross in 400 yards. Here turn right, northwards into Dean Lane, and follow the path between double hedges. If this is still closed you will have to keep to the tarred road, onwards to Ellicombe in a mile where you turn right and then right again. Hopefully, you will be able to cut off this corner by going over the hill, heading towards the dome at Butlin's, Minehead, and descend to the road in 700 yards. With the old quarries to your left, drop down to the medieval shoreline of the Bristol Channel where it is said King Stephen found the castle defended on one side by the sea and on the other by battlements.

Turn right at the lane, eastwards towards the sound of the traffic, for 250 yards. Then turn left, at the junction, and turn right for 50 yards, along the verge beside the main road. Cross the A39 at the junction signed to Marsh Street. You are heading for Dunster Station and Dunster Beach.

The Yarn Market is the distinctive and picturesque building in the High Street

Turn left at Marsh Street in 300 yards. Proceed straight ahead at the junction with Sea Lane in 100 yards. Dunster Station is in 250 yards, where in summertime you may have timed it right for a short steam excursion into Minehead, as the train usually changes direction and returns about half an hour later. Beyond the railway the road becomes a track at Lower Marsh Farm and leads to a patch of scrubland where you join the coastal path in 1000 yards. Turn right here, south-eastwards beside The Hawn lagoon to the car park at Sea Lane End in another 1000 yards. Turn right beside a wartime pillbox camouflaged with beach pebbles. Head westwards along Sea Lane, back across the railway, to the junction at Marsh Street in 1000 yards.

Turn left at the junction, over the bridge, and then left again at the second junction in 150 yards. You pass Marsh Cider Cottage and come to the 1858-dated police station beside the main road (and the modern Coppers) in 300 yards. Turn left along the pavement and go under the subway in 100 yards. Cross to the opposite pavement in 50 yards. Turn right and return to Dunster, reaching the historic Luttrell Arms and Yarn Market in 400 yards and the slope up into Dunster Castle at the other end of the High Street in another 300 yards. Bear left to return to the car park in 200 yards.

Gallox Bridge is a medieval packhorse bridge beside a ford

The war memorial, at the seaward end of Higher Town, Minehead

20

MINEHEAD AND BURGUNDY

Exmoor begins with a heavily wooded headland of red sandstone as the backdrop to Minehead. Much of this wild landscape, along Culver Cliff and into Moor Wood, has been bought by the National Park Authority, and the National Trust acquired cliff-side pastures at Greenaleigh Point in 1985. Paths hereabouts become almost too much of a good thing with a confusion of options that almost defies description. You also have to be prepared for cul-de-sac adventures and to go into reverse as a track that looks inviting turns into a nightmare. One such option, signed down North Hill to Burgundy Chapel, became an exercise in damage limitation as the author found himself entangled in brambles, tripping over rocks, and sliding across the slime of a gushing springline.

Circuits for public consumption have to be more selective. Never easily accessible, Burgundy is still a special place, with the mystery and magic of somewhere sacred and secret. Not much is left of its earliest medieval domestic building – perhaps a hermitage – which was set on a narrow platform between the cliff, a stream, and the sea. Immediately east of it is another rectangle of sandstone rubble, about 13 feet wide by 30 feet long, with a finely carved doorway in its single surviving wall.

A lone wall is almost all that survives of Burgundy Chapel

This was a medieval chapel, dedicated to the Holy Trinity, which has been attributed to an otherwise unknown member of the Luttrell family in thanks for his safe return from the Burgundian War in the fourteenth century. These details are related on a sign beside the chapel. In fact the main conflicts in Burgundy were a little later, after 1404, when John the Fearless joined English invaders and was implicated in the assassination of the Duke of Orleans. John himself was to be assassinated, in 1419, during a period when England won most of the battles but lost the war. By 1450 we had been evicted from all of France apart from Calais (and its supermarkets).

Minehead's other treasure, in beautiful Gothic script, is behind protective glass in St Michael's Parish Church at Higher Town. It is the illuminated Missal of Richard Fitzjames who was the town's vicar. He went on to be Bishop of London from 1506 until his death in 1522. The hand-written volume of masses and sacraments pre-dates him by several decades. The clue to its dating is that St Anne's Day is shown in red

Elgin Tower, in Scottish baronial style, looks out to sea

Jack the Hammer has his bell but lacks the rest of the striking mechanism

lettering. Anne was reduced in status to a black-letter saint when the Vatican reformed its Kalendar in 1350. The return to Minehead of the Fitzjames Missal was in almost miraculous circumstances as it was bought at auction, from Sotheby's in 1949, and donated to the town by Cecil Henry Bullivant. Its thousand pages of vellum contain the lifetime's scribing of more than one monk.

The church also has its colourful bell-ringer. Jack Hammer, the personalised clock-striking mechanism who now lacks his dial, is mentioned in the churchwardens' accounts for 1641. 'Strikingly situated', to quote its guide, the tower of St Michael's Church is the town's major landmark. It reaches up towards the woods behind it. Around it is the historic cottage corner of Minehead which overlooks a harbour that was the contemporary of both. This was one of the premier ports of the West Country. Visually and historically it was the Somerset equivalent of the famous Cobb at Lyme Regis. Both retain their lifeboat stations. Minehead has even managed to save its branch railway, thanks to help from Butlin's, which almost makes it the Swanage of the Bristol Channel. A 4-mile circuit brings in the harbour, church, wooded hill and Burgundy Chapel.

THE WALK

Approach Minehead along the A39. Park and start from the northern part of the sea front (SS 971 471). Set off along Quay Street, towards the harbour, and pass the marvellously named Old Ship Aground, followed by the 1901-dated lifeboat station. Continue for the length of Quay West.

The last house is Sea Crest, after which you join a public bridleway, to Greenaleigh Farm. The track follows the bottom edge of the woods, above beachside lawns, north-westwards. It goes through the sycamores and rhododendrons of Culver Cliff Wood in half a mile. On reaching the pastures above and beyond Culver Cliff Sand you enter National Trust land.

The unpaved road brings you to Greenaleigh Farm, a mile into your walk, and you continue straight ahead for a further half-mile. You are heading for the remains of Burgundy Chapel, one of Somerset's remotest romantic ruins, on the far side of deep-cut and landslipped Burgundy Chapel Combe.

From here, turn around and retrace your steps to Greenaleigh Farm. Continue for just 50 yards beyond it, towards Minehead, and then turn right. A sunken trackway up through the trees, heading south-eastwards, is signed for North Hill. Proceed straight ahead at a minor crossroads of woodland tracks and then do the same at a more

Wedding-cake skyline of Butlin's modernised holiday-land at Minehead

conspicuous one beside the seat to Colin and Mary Cozens. Turn right at the next junction of tracks, uphill, and then fork left at the following offering of tracks. You will still be heading upwards and approach a hilly pasture, 500 yards from Greenaleigh Farm, with a view across Minehead Bay to the coast beyond Blue Anchor.

In 300 yards you descend southwards through birch woodland to a crossroads of tracks to the right of a cattle-grid and gate. North Hill is signed to the right. Take neither of these paths but instead continue straight ahead in what is signed as the 'Woodland Walk'. The track through Moor Wood bends to the left, through the sweet chestnuts, and zigzags in its descent south-eastwards towards the Higher Town district of Minehead.

In 500 yards, on the far side of Moor Wood, you come to a narrow pasture with woods on either side. Head towards a glimpse of the Quantock Hills with the railway line in the middle distance. According to the map there is a public bridleway along the left side of this wedge of grassland. There is also a permissive path, across a stile beside a gate, which runs just inside the right-hand wooded slope. The two paths converge on the far side of the pasture in 350 yards.

Continue straight ahead, down a dirt road, for a further 200 yards. Turn left on emerging at the tarred road – away from Higher Moor – and fork left at the next corner, after Somerset Riding Centre and Hillside Barn. In 500 yards you come to the parish church, with its tower and sloping churchyard perched on a high red wall above the cobbles and thatch of Church Steps.

Follow St Michael's Road eastwards for 250 yards to the Scottish baronial-style mansion, on the corner with Burgundy Road, and the war memorial. Continue straight ahead into the cul-de-sac of Weirfield Road. At the end, in 50 yards, a footpath continues straight ahead from the right-hand side of the drive to Green Gables and brings you to a junction of paths at the top of the wooded cliffs.

Turn right here, and then left in another 50 yards, for the final descent through the pines. Turn left at the bottom, beside a sign for the South West Coast Path. Opened in 1975, the country's longest long-distance route officially runs for 515 miles – to Land's End and Poole Harbour – but users insist that 541 miles is a more accurate estimate. Your onward path is a little less ambitious. In a few yards you emerge on the promenade, beside the thatch of Seagate Cottage, and are back in Quay Street.

Minehead at the end of the line (centre) *which is still in steam*

Whitewashed walls of the cottages beside Church Steps

Cream-coloured cottages cluster around Selworthy Green

21

SELWORTHY AND HOLNICOTE

Tenants were puzzled, and members of his family stunned, when 15th Baronet Sir Richard Acland went through a political transformation and gave his entire 17,000-acre estates at Holnicote and Killerton to the National Trust in 1944. Having been the Liberal MP for North Devon since 1935, he had launched his own party with a public ownership agenda. Those attracted to the cause included Sir Oswald Mosley's deputy, Robert Forgan, who made his last public speech for Acland's Common Wealth Party in the 1945 general election. Sir Richard failed to be elected, in Putney, but then reinvented himself as a Fabian socialist and was returned by Gravesend, for Labour, in its 1947 by-election.

Selworthy's whitewashed church overlooks the valley

Nowhere were the estate workers more baffled than at Selworthy, which had been established as a model village for retired servants and staff, in a cluster of picturesque thatched cottages high on the south-facing hills between Minehead and Porlock. A generation later, one of them chatted to the author in the woods after woodpeckers stopped drumming and a pheasant cried out, a second before the air cracked with a thud and rumble at 17.45 hours. The gentleman, approaching with his dog, must have realised how startling it was.

'That's Concorde, going to New York,' he explained. 'On a clearer day you'd be able to see her. You can tell the time by them.' He went on to talk about the repercussions of the 1944 takeover of Selworthy by the National Trust. 'We exchanged one feudal landlord for another – how on earth could anyone be so enthralled by London life to decide to give all this away? Everything, for as far as you can see, and a lot more that you can't!'

Exmoor ponies on Bratton Ball

Protected from the gales by the wooded shoulder of a coastal beacon, and claiming to be the most beautiful village in England, Selworthy overlooks the family's Somerset seat at Holnicote House. This mansion replaced 'the noble old manor of Sir Thomas Acland' which was destroyed by fire in 1779. The next Sir Thomas – the 10th Baronet – created Selworthy as we admire it today. Despite a large hillside church, and an exceptionally crowded churchyard, there were few houses in the village in 1828 when Sir Thomas

Mausoleum style for the Acland family's memorial hut

Bow Cottage at Selworthy

decided to build it as a model hamlet. He was so intrigued by something similar at Blaise Hamlet, Henbury, near Bristol, that he designed it 'as a refuge for estate pensioners'.

Building the collection of matching chocolate-box cottages provided a workfare project for those times of agricultural deprivation. They were made available to the staff and retainers on their retirement, as they are to this day, for the Trust still looks after its own, although no longer rent-free. The Acland family also enhanced the estate with a series of viewpoint resting places. All Saints' Parish Church also has the Acland name writ large. Apart from the memorials, look up to the comfortable south-facing upper storey over the porch, which was their balcony pew.

Architecturally impressive is the 45-feet-high embattled tower of about 1400. It is painted, like the cottages, but with a purer white than the ubiquitous National Trust cream. The mechanism of the hour-striking clock is a couple of centuries earlier than the walls. An octagonal ancient stone bowl, found in a hedgebank half a mile east at Howe's Close, is carved with two primitive Celtic faces on opposite sides and alternating with a couple of simple crosses. Said to have been from the site of a Saxon or Viking burial mound, it may well be one of the oldest fonts in the country.

Outside, the church retains its medieval churchyard cross, somewhat weathered but otherwise in remarkably fine condition. Surrounded by dozens of clean-carved gravestones, it is 12 feet high and comprises an hexagonal three-stepped plinth, decorated square base, and chamfered shaft.

THE WALK
Selworthy offers a delightful 4-mile walk. Approach the village by turning north from the A39, near Holnicote House, half a mile east of Allerford. You come to thatched cottages, a steep hill, and the church in half a mile. Continue up the lane for a further 100 yards and then turn right into the National Trust car park (SS 922 468).

Set off by returning to the church and war memorial at the corner above Selworthy Green in 100 yards. Turn right here, northwards through the gate, and follow the main path beside the stream. In 400 yards, up the wooded combe, you fork left across the stream on to a lesser path towards Selworthy Beacon and Bury Castle, an Iron Age settlement. Stone-walled banks to the left mark a medieval farmstead.

In half a mile the rocky path rises above the tree-line of beech and pine, above a walled spring, with gorse-covered moorland to the right. Then in 120 yards, to your left under the last of the pines, you pass the memorial hut to Sir Thomas Acland (1787–1871). It was built like a mausoleum, in red sandstone, on a spot chosen by his youngest surviving son, John Barton Arundel Acland – of Holnicote, New Zealand – in 1878. Inscriptions include Keble on the 'deepening glen', and Hever on the 'beauty seen' gilding 'the span of ruin'd earth and sinful man'.

From here you continue across the road, north-eastwards along a dirt track, to a cairn on the skyline in 500 yards. Placed at 1012 feet above sea level, this is Selworthy Beacon – the Acland family's twin peak – partnered by Dunkery Beacon to the south, with the latter being the highest point in Somerset. It gives a classic view of the Bristol Channel, along the Devon and Somerset coast from Foreland Point to Steep Holm island, with the much of the South Wales seaboard spread out ahead of you.

Turn up-Channel, eastwards along the stony track, heading towards Steep Holm and what little you can see of Minehead. The sea is to your left. In 500 yards the path descends to a road where you turn left, south-eastwards, for 200 yards. On the other side of the bend you turn right, southwards towards Selworthy, and follow the path down the slope to a crossroads of rough tracks in 150 yards. Again turn right and descend south-westwards into the woods of Selworthy Combe in 600 yards.

Here there is a diversion from the main path, westwards along a lesser path for 150 yards, up to Lady Acland's Hut. This summer house, in a fairytale setting, was erected in about 1879 for Lady Gertrude Acland, wife of 12th Baronet Sir Charles Acland. It was restored in 1954 by the National Trust and is 'open to all for rest and shelter during daylight hours'. It is a timber chalet, with an attractive circular chimney, but the fireplace has been bricked up.

Walk down the slope for about 50 yards to the three former ponds, behind a series of stout dams, which are now semi-drained and covered with trees. Turn right along the path and follow it and the stream, beneath the big redwood, down to the little bridge in 100 yards. Here you turn right on rejoining the main track. Follow it and the stream for 600 yards down into Selworthy.

After going through the gate, climb the flight of steps to the stone stile beneath the churchyard yew for the perfect view of the chocolate-box village. Then walk back through the churchyard to the far gate and return to your car.

Piles Mill serviced the Holnicote Estate

Mill machinery worked an apple-crusher for cider making

Rising tide leaving three splashes of Selworthy Sand still to be inundated

22

BOSSINGTON AND HURLSTONE

Exmoor makes its best plunge towards the sea in a rugged and romantic corner of the 12,443-acre Holnicote Estate to the east of Porlock. This is the first point since Minehead where roads and footpaths come within spitting distance of the Bristol Channel. The approach is via the delightfully picturesque villages of Allerford and Bossington, plus a Farm Park and Birds of Prey Centre beside a medieval chapel at Lynch, as you follow the wooded escarpment around the valley floor from the A39 west of Selworthy.

The great westward panorama is into Devon, to the silhouettes of Old Burrow and Foreland Point. Moorland vegetation gives way to maritime flora of the Atlantic seaboard. So, too, does the bird life, with circling buzzards and croaking ravens, then jackdaws and razorbills. Deer slots are there to be noticed, if not the actual creatures, and this is very much a place where architecture trails the wildlife. Exmoor also does well with rare breeds.

Coastguard station, now roofless, on Hurlstone Point

Look out for Devon Closewool sheep and North Devon cattle, nicknamed the Red Ruby, as taken to America by the Pilgrim Fathers. Exmoor ponies are unique. It is the archetypal Celtic horse, hardly changed since the Ice Age, which was granted rare breed status in 1981. No other horse has this direct connection with pre-history. It proves that Iron Age warriors were much smaller than modern males as both mares and stallions are under 12.3 hands (124 centimetres). There were only 50 Exmoor ponies at the end of the Second World War but 200 now roam the moor and there are another 1000 dispersed worldwide.

THE WALK

The circuit for a 4-mile walk is based on Bossington. Park and start in the National Trust car park which you enter between Wayside, Kitnors and the Orchard Guest House (SS 898 480). Set off on the 'Bridleway to Hurlstone Point'. This crosses the river at North Bridge and you then turn left along the track which follows the river for a short stretch downstream. Then it forks right, upwards along the side of Bossington Hill, as you head northwards. After the chalet you descend towards the sea but then bear right, through a gate, to climb through open ground beside Hurlstone Combe in half a mile. Look down on the bank of pebbles to the left which cover the mouth of Horner Water.

The last grass on the Holnicote Estate between Bossington and the sea

North Bridge links Bossington with the coastal path

Ancient chapel beside the Farm Park at Lynch

In flash-floods 'it bursts up through the pebbles with a tremendous roar', to quote a National Trust information panel.

Around you the vegetation grows wilder. The hollyhocks of the cottage gardens give way to greater mullein and foxgloves. Further up the windward slopes, above the scree, are expanses of heather moorland and dwarf gorse. At the National Trust's omega-shaped sign for 'Hurlstone' – beside which is an emergency coastguard telephone – you are given two options. Take heed of any warning but for now proceed straight ahead to see the gaunt shell of the former coastguard station on Hurlstone Point. Around the Victorian stone blockhouse the headland is smothered with pink thrift and a miniature species of stonecrop.

If the coast path is open and usable you can cross a stile and turn right on the exposed slopes to zigzag up to the northern lip of Hurlstone Combe. A safer alternative is to return to the omega sign and walk up the middle of the combe, along the strip of grass between the bracken. The two paths meet at the top of the combe, half a mile south-east of the coastguard station.

From here, keep your back to the sea and take the coast path uphill towards Minehead. Across to your right is the cairn at 800 feet on Bossington Hill which is a popular place for parascending. As you continue inland you cross and climb a great tract of open moor. In half a mile, at a pointer, you turn right and head westwards towards the inner cove of Porlock Bay.

You are now going downhill and pass a long embankment which seems to be associated with Second World War defences or training targets. An underground bunker at the opposite end has been sealed with concrete. In 200 yards you pass a path junction and then turn left on to another path in 15 yards. This second path goes out on to a bracken-clad spur as you head south-westwards towards the inundated meadows between Porlock town and Porlock Bay.

On the outcrop in 300 yards the path suddenly bends leftward, south-eastwards, to face the side of a wood on the opposite slopes of a deep-cut valley. As you turn you look down on the hamlet of Lynch, with its sixteenth-century chapel incorporated into the main barn of a later farmyard at Park Farm. In 300 yards, at the seat in Lynch Combe, take the first turning on the right.

This heads westwards towards the wood. Cross a little stream and follow the rocky path through the outer belt of trees on 200 yards. Keep the wall of the main wood to your left and ignore the paths into it, taking the one for Lynch which follows the outer wall down the valley floor. Also ignore a second gate, to your left, and likewise another to the right. The main track continues downhill, now between two walls, to a gate beside a field in 350 yards.

Here, at a National Trust sign, you leave Selworthy Woods and then turn right into a field in 50 yards. Pass the site of a sheep-dip and walk north-westwards along the lynchet (a ridge left from ancient ploughing on a slope) that gives Lynch its name. Admire a couple of walnut trees. On entering the next field in 200 yards you turn left, towards Bossington, and follow the fence downhill for 50 yards to a hunting gate in the corner, beside a holly bush.

Descend to the oak tree in five yards and then turn right after the three steps below it. You will now be walking above the river which you can hear and glimpse to the left. On going through a kissing gate, bear left and cross the river at a ford and footbridge in 45 yards. The gate on the other side is into the National Trust car park

Chocolate-box idyll in Bossington hamlet

The Pack Horse (right) *and bridge at Allerford*

Hurlstone Point juts out into Porlock Bay

23

PORLOCK AND PORLOCK WEIR

Porlock's primary claim to fame is that newly-hooked opium addict Samuel Taylor Coleridge, recalling the sunny pleasure-dome of Xanadu for his dream-poem 'Kubla Khan', was interrupted by the unexpected arrival of a 'person from Porlock' who turned out to be an insurance salesman. It caused him to forget the remaining hypnagogic imagery of what he subtitled 'A Vision in a Dream'. That incident happened in Nether Stowey in 1799. There has also been excitement since, such as the hauling over the hill of the Lynmouth Lifeboat for an heroic rescue against the odds, and a moment of triumph in the Battle of Britain.

Pilot Officer Eric 'Boy' Marrs in a Spitfire of 152 Squadron from RAF Warmwell, having crippled a Junkers bomber, allowed it to make a successful forced landing on the beach at Porlock. He swept low over the shore as the crew left the aircraft and waved to him in thanks. Less happily, a nearby memorial commemorates 11 United States airmen who were killed when their Liberator bomber crashed on returning from a U-boat patrol over the Bay of Biscay on 29 October 1942.

Porlock also boasts a hill with lamentable PR. It is a fearsome zigzag with a 1-in-4 gradient. The poet Robert Southey found it a hill too far after calling on Coleridge in 1799: 'Porlock is called in the neighbourhood "The End of the World". All beyond is inaccessible to carriage or even cart.'

Porlock Hill's conquest by the motor car took place in August 1900, winning Selwyn Francis Edge a £50 wager when he reached the top in his 1.6 horsepower Napier. It is said that this and other early vehicles went up backwards. The cartoonist Sir Francis Carruthers Gould, who retired to Porlock in 1914, passed on the legend:

Early motors had gravity-fed petrol pipes and had to go up in reverse. But they lacked the power to carry the driver as well. So he locked the throttle, jumped out, and steered from the outside.

That is in the past, since the hill was tarred in 1930, though it remains formidable. There was a water-tank for those with boiling radiators and the old AA post is now listed as

Exotic leaves spilling into the road from sub-tropical Chapel Knap Gardens overlooking Porlock Bay

The main harbour at Porlock Weir is below the Pieces of Eight Tea Room

The Drang is the historic alleyway running alongside Porlock churchyard

an historic building. Down in the town, Doverhay Court dates from 1450, and was regentrified in Victorian times. It is now Dovery Manor Museum managed by Dennis Corner. Nearby, the cottage ornée look predominates, at and around The Gables. Across the main street, St Dubricius Parish Church is named for a post-Roman archbishop who is reputed to have married King Arthur and Queen Guinevere. An ancient yew shadows the tower with an oak-shingled spire which has had an unfinished look since the top was blown off and taken, it is said, to Culbone. The Chantry – where its priests lived – stands across The Drang, the West Country dialect word for an alleyway. They were endowed to pray for the ancestors and soul of John, Lord Harrington, who died in 1428 and resides as an alabaster effigy.

Porlock's medieval port, at Porlock Weir, is largely high and dry. *The Democrat* was the last coaster to call, delivering coal in 1931, and the harbour mouth has since been blocked by pebbles. Further east, however, there is a submarine forest and the sea has reasserted itself, having broken through the shingle beside Decoy Lagoon and flooded low-lying meadows in the tail of Hurricane Lily on the night of 28 October 1996. It is a commendable example of 'managed retreat' in which nature thrives as maritime plants and birds return to a half-mile deep marshland buffer zone between the beach and the town. National Trust land lies to one side and Sparkhayes Lane now ends in a swamp. The dynamic habitat improvement has seen wildlife performing on a scale unknown in living memory. It has come too late, however, for the auroch. Its bones, found on the foreshore at Porlock, date from 2000BC in the Bronze Age. These huge and primitive wild cattle became extinct before recorded history.

When the poet Robert Southey visited Porlock he stayed at the Ship Inn, in a room that was almost en suite, with 'a decent pot de chamber and no fleas'. Pearce's Tannery, since demolished, was the training base for the riding team which won equestrian gold in the Olympic Games of 1952. British hopefuls of the following half-century have attended the riding stables at Porlock Ford House. The Forge, in Doverhay, used to be the busiest farriery in Britain but now sends vans to its equine clientele rather than having them clopping into Porlock tó be reshod.

Crossing the breach in the shingle

THE WALK

Porlock would be an excellent place for a simple 4-mile walk apart from the potentially dangerous breakthrough of the sea across the pebble beach east of Porlock Weir. Observe warning signs as this is currently impassable at high tide; a safe alternative is given below. Having approached Porlock on the A39 between Minehead and Lynmouth, park and start in Doverhay car park, on the eastern side of the town (SS 888 467).

Set off westwards along the High Street, beside the 1704-dated Royal Oak and Lorna Doone Hotel, and pass The Countryman. Bear right beside the thatched Old Rose and Crown, opposite the Parish Church of St Dubricius and The Drang alleyway. Having passed the Post Office and 1604-dated Myrtle Cottage, take the second turning on the right, just up from the Ship Inn, which is signed beside the Village Hall as the 'Toll Road – Scenic Route' to Lynmouth, through Porlock Manor Estate.

Fork right in 350 yards, after Elthorne, which is the last house on the left, along a stony double-hedged lane signed to the coast path. You now have a view over the Decoy Lagoon and Porlock Bay, across the Bristol Channel to South Wales. After Park House and Greencombe the woodland track skirts Allerpark Combe and brings you almost into West Porlock hamlet in a mile. Here you turn left, uphill along the 'Horses to Porlock Weir' option. Then in 100 yards, turn left again, continuing uphill, along a stony gully through clumps of fern. In 75 yards you come to a woodland crossroads. Turn right,

The Old Rose and Crown, a former hostelry, faces Porlock parish church

The historic but silted inner haven at Porlock Weir

Classic car taking little carriageway as it passes the Royal Oak in Porlock

downwards, again following the arrow for 'Horses to Porlock Weir'. By now you will be thinking that you should have brought your horse! You descend into Hawknest Combe.

Having crossed the stream the track then follows it down to the road. Cross to the woodland path on the other side and drop down to the next road, beside Mariners Combe. In 75 yards you turn left, along the toll road to Worthy. This takes you through the upper settlement of Porlock Weir, beside exotic Chapel Knap Gardens and the corrugated iron mission church of St Nicholas.

Below the range of thatched cottages you fork left, uphill, towards Worthy. Pass the veritable botanical collection at Ivystone. Then pass Owls Combe. In 300 yards, immediately before Worthy Manor, turn sharply right down the slope to Porlock Weir. You are now heading east, with the sea to your left, and the path brings you to a pasture above the dock, groynes and quay in 500 yards. Turn left at the end of this field, down the flight of steps, to the road between The Kiln and Shingle Ridge workshops. The track to the left passes the historic inner harbour. To the right, your onward route passes the Pieces of Eight Tea Room and the Anchor Hotel. Fork left at the Ship Inn, keeping to the seaward road which leaves the thatched sector of Porlock Weir hamlet between Gibraltar Cottage and Beach Cottage. After the houses the road bends inland and you turn left, down a flight of steps, to the beach. Turn right along the shingle towards Hurlstone Point.

Observe warning signs because at the time of writing the sea floods through a breach in the pebbles at high tide – into the Decoy Lagoon and across its marshes – and is also potentially dangerous as it flows out, across beds of exposed clay. If and when there is a safe way across, though it may only be usable at low tide, you can proceed for half a mile to the memorial to airmen killed when their Liberator bomber crashed here in 1942.

Then the coast path enters the north-western extremity of the National Trust's Holnicote Estate. In 200 yards you turn right, southwards, to join the path on or beside Sparkhayes Lane which heads into Porlock. If, however, the sea has broken through the beach you will have to take an alternative route after leaving Porlock Weir. Instead you turn right 400 yards along the beach, beside the oaks after the riding school paddocks. Carry on under a power line at the northern end of Porlockford Plantation.

The path then follows the hedgerow, which is to your right, south-easterly for 800 yards. It then turns right, into Courtmead Lane, which brings you to the B3225 in 300 yards. Turn left along the road, for the final mile, back into Porlock.

Sheep penning in the coastal pasture above The Kiln

Porlock Bay and the Decoy Lagoon from Porlock Hill

24

CULBONE AND WORTHY COMBE

Exquisite Culbone, deep in dense woods on Exmoor's coastal slope, claims to be 'the smallest complete church in England'. It is also almost unique as a place out of bounds to motor vehicles, its only access being on foot. Another rarity is the dedication, to Saint Beuno, who founded the monastery at Clodoch in the Black Mountains and was laid to rest on Bardsey – 'the Isle of the Saints' off Snowdonia – in about AD623.

Dairy farms between Culbone Hill and the coast

The tiny Celtic community at Culbone in Saxon times was known as *Cyta-Ore* for the 'cave by the sea' which became corrupted as 'Kitnor' in the Middle Ages. By then its isolation had attracted refugees. They had created an 'enclosure' in 1265 which became a prison camp from 1385 to 1450. The next batch of outcasts established a leper colony from 1544 until 1622. This accounts for the leper-squint window in the north side of the nave in the miniature church to enable them to attend Mass from outside in the churchyard.

Finally, the valley became the home for 38 prisoners of war, captured in 1720 whilst fighting for the French in India. They remained for twenty-one years. Several then turned down the possibility of returning home and continued to work as charcoal burners and bark-strippers, in these cliff-hanging woods, to produce raw materials for leather tanning. The substance stained their bodies and gave them an English name, while the churchyard became a burying ground, almost exclusively, for members of the Red family. The oldest surviving stone is to John Red, who died in 1832, and the most recent is to Irving and Ethel Red who both died in 1966. One hopes he picked the obvious words when he proposed to her: 'Are you ready to become Ethelred?'

The handful of other names include James Court of Ashley Combe:

For more than sixty years woodman and faithful friend to the first and second Earls of Lovelace and to Mary Countess of Lovelace.

Culbone has the smallest complete church in the country

Measurements are material to the Culbone story. The church has a chancel 13 feet 6 inches long by 10 feet wide with a thirteenth-century chancel arch. It opens into a nave 21 feet 6 inches long by 12 feet 4 inches across. The walls are 2 feet thick. An anchorite's cell is

Standing stones, apparently recent, on Porlock Common

Pagan cartwheel converted into Christian cross on the Culbone Stone

set in the north side of the chancel. Its two-light window, carved from a single block of faded red sandstone, is 2 feet wide and has the primitive outline of a head incised on the outside, at the top, between the two arched slits. The font is Norman.

Topping off the roof is a dainty spire, added in 1810, which is said to have come from Porlock church tower, after it had been blown down in a storm. Beneath are two small bells, including a 'long-waisted' early-fourteenth-century specimen which is the earliest bell in West Somerset.

Others have enthused over Culbone and its 'utter solitude'. Sir Nikolaus Pevsner described it as 'delightful, with the rushing stream, the screen of wooded hillside and the distant corner of the sea' and was enchanted by 'the little slate spire riding on the nave roof, and the whitewash having come off in irregular patches to expose rubble stone underneath'.

En route to Culbone you have a chance to stop and stroll into a ragged wood of dwarf pines to see a reddish 2-feet-high standing stone. The Culbone Stone, close to the parish boundary, is carved with an incised wheeled cross which is a ballot-paper type 'X' set in a circle of hand-sized diameter.

This has been claimed as a sixth-century Christian carving but it may pre-date that and be a Celtic cartwheel motif from the Iron Age. The evidence for this is that the 'X' of the circle has an outward line extending from the bottom right which was added later, apparently to 'Christianise' a pagan stone. The extended incision is less deep than the design inside the circle and twice the width of the other lines. Either way, it is a romantic stone, in a wild place. There are also several rows of uninscribed stones stretching outwards from the wood into the bracken beyond.

THE WALK

For a 5-mile circuit of Culbone and its woods, turn north from the A39 opposite Culbone Stables Inn which is 3 miles west from the cattle-grid on the summit of Porlock Hill. After turning off the main road you cross another cattle-grid and then pass a lay-by with a short waymarked path to the Culbone Stone.

Our walk begins a mile further down the road, from a crossroads with signs to Porlock Weir, Silcombe Farm, Yarner Farm and Ash Farm (SS 848 476). Set off north-westwards, uphill and then downhill, to Ash Farm in half a mile.

Next is Parsonage Farm where the road bends to the right at a catalpa tree and then goes left and uphill, above Withy Combe woods and stream. From here you climb again, with a panoramic view of the South Wales coast, and in 400 yards you approach Silcombe Farm. Turn right as it comes into sight, northwards, along the path that runs eastwards to Culbone and Porlock Weir. Descend to a gate but then ignore the main track into the woods. Instead, turn abruptly right, southwards, along a narrow and stony alternative path that drops down into the trees. It follows a stream and brings you to a house in 200 yards.

Fork right on approaching the main arch and pass under a second ivy-clad arch – beside a waterfall – beyond which, in 50 yards, you come to the churchyard with its lines of head-stones to the Red family of Broomstreet. Leave the Culbone churchyard through the gate beyond the nave and spire. Then turn left and go left again on reaching the house. Follow signs for Porlock Weir.

This points you up and over the arched bridge and you then go left again on the other side, along a path which is liable to carry safety warnings of 'unstable ground' and potential land-slips. If the path has been closed for safety reasons you will have to turn round and follow the 'Alternative Route' back to your car.

Assuming the path is open, continue eastwards. These delightful woods are a mixture of species including sweet chestnut, mountain ash, and the occasional strawberry tree, among the standard Exmoor offering of sessile oaks. The roar of the sea takes over from the babble of the stream.

For half a mile carry on climbing along a terraced path. Then you fork left and descend for the next half-mile. Keep on the main track (or follow any 'Alternative Route' to Porlock Weir). The historic track zigzags left and then right on the last leg, via steps, and goes through arches beneath a fort-like folly.

You reach the tarred road at a semi-circular thatched toll-house which is the pay-gate for 'Worthy Combe Toll Road'. Turn left and then go straight ahead, away from the gate, for 100 yards. Just before Worthy Manor, turn right up a path signed to Yearnor Mill Bridge. This bridleway ascends Withy Combe, following the stream south-westwards for half a mile, then follow the blue arrows. There is a road across to your right on the other side of the stream.

Pass Yearnor Mill. In 100 yards, you come to the edge of the wood where you should turn right at the fence-line, heading towards Culbone. In 50 yards the track bends to the right and bridges the stream. Turn left at the tarred road and walk uphill for 250 yards. Turn sharply right at the junction, north-eastwards, towards Countisbury and Lynmouth. The road bends across the hill and brings you back to your crossroads starting point in 700 yards.

Rainbow over Porlock's coastal hinterland

Curving walls of the thatched pay-gate on the Worthy Combe Toll Road

Fiction merges with fact at Lorna Doone Farm beside Malmsmead Bridge

25

DOONE COUNTRY AND OARE

Publication in 1869 of *Lorna Doone* made an impact on the Victorian romantic imagination as potent as that of Wordsworth and his Lakeland daffodils on an earlier generation. Coinciding with the arrival of the railways it introduced a newly accessible wilderness to a national clientele. Richard Doddridge Blackmore did for Exmoor what Sir Walter Scott had achieved for the Highlands. Those who ridicule 'Lorna Doonery'– as it was dubbed by Sir William Halliday – will think this ludicrous but it could be argued that he was the saviour of Doone Country rather than merely having created it. Returning to the car after yet another drenching, the thought occurs that the record-breaking rainfall makes this the perfect place for a reservoir. Without Doonery it would be a nowhere ripe for despoilation.

Until the designation of Exmoor National Park in 1954, linking the highlands of Somerset and Devon, the uninhabited landscape south of County Gate lay in a no-man's-land on the borderlands. The approach is from Malmsmead in Somerset but the historical lost location to which it leads is Badgworthy in Devon. Fiction merging with fact happens all the way, via a Lorna Doone Hotel in Porlock, and Lorna Doone Farm beside medieval Malmsmead Bridge. Lorna Doone Ridd and three generations of John Ridds have their gravestones at Martinhoe. You will see a life-size statue of Lorna, by Professor George Stephenson, if you start your exploration of Exmoor from beside the police station in Dulverton.

On the high heartland of the story there is nothing much that could be renamed in her memory, other than the all-embracing Doone Country tag which the Ordnance Survey now validates. Valleys and moors converge around a deserted street at Badgworthy where a cluster of cottages has been reduced to heaps of stones in the bracken. It is a mile-and-a-half south of Lorna Doone Farm, above Holcombe tributary on the Devon side of the surging Badgworthy Water, just beyond stunted oaks festooned with ferns, in the humid micro-climate of the wettest spots in the West Country.

The tree-line fails to climb beyond the protection of the lower valley. Just one stony cart-track, now a bridleway, leads into it. En route there is a wayside memorial to the

Cloud Farm is the closest inhabitation to deserted Doone Country

Robber's Bridge is a reminder that this was brigand country

aforementioned Blackmore whose novel 'extols to all the world the joys of Exmoor'. It was provided by the Lorna Doone Centenary Committee in 1969. Badgworthy is the land of the brigands to which Blackmore's hero rides to the rescue in the seventeenth century. Just finding Oare can be hard enough, as its isolationary jingle implies:

Culbone, Oare and Stoke Pero,
Parishes three no parson'll go to.
Culbone, Oare and Stoke Pero,
Three such places you'll seldom hear o'.

Oare was almost tame compared with the legends that attached to Badgworthy. Scenic and idyllic, in an oasis of green, the latter was in a league of its own when it came to standards of behaviour, even in a brutalised age. The Doones were firmly emplaced in folklore:

Child, if they ask who killed thee,
Say it was the Doones of Badgworthy.

Badgworthy Water flows down from the high moors

Mossy rocks and white-water at Badgworthy

Blackmore had access to the parish records on the Somerset side of Badgworthy Water and was aware of at least one instance of real-life outlawry. Walter, a chaplain there in the Middle Ages, was murdered by Robert of Oare, in an incident which left the chaplain's son, Gervase, maimed with sword cuts. Oare, as a Domesday village of some significance, has a watery name in sound and on the ground, as it is directly derived from the Celtic name for its river, the 'Are'. Next up its valley is Robber's Bridge. It was an accident of history that a rector's grandson should have stumbled upon the magic and mystery of inner Exmoor, He proceeded to put everlasting life into the legend of stock-raiders and highway robbers from the Scottish Borders, who found refuge here during post-medieval turbulence, in an already crumbling Badgworthy. Persevering in their old ways they would eventually provoke an uprising among the good people of Exmoor.

Blackmore's alter ego – given 29 November 1661 for his date of birth – was located at Plover's Barrow, which is another lost place-name, on the hilltop above Oare House:

> *If anyone cares to read a simple tale, told simply, I, John Ridd, of the parish of Oare in the county of Somerset, yeoman and churchwarden, have seen and had a share in some doings of this neighbourhood, which I will try and set down in order, God preserving my life and memory.*

A grim total of 34 men, women and children died in the Lynmouth flood disaster on Friday 15 August 1952. Exmoor had already received 6 inches of rain that month, saturating the ground, and the death toll would have been higher but for the number of holidaymakers who cancelled their vacations and went home earlier in the week. Incessant rain resumed at lunchtime on the fateful Friday, with some 9 inches falling on the hills that funnel water into Lynmouth's narrow gorge, and feed other catchments. By 5pm both arms of the swollen River Lyn were threatening properties. At 6pm the Tors footbridge was swept away, followed by May Bridge as the debris reached the harbour. Utilities began to fail at 8pm when the hydro-electric power station of Lynmouth Electric Light Company had too much of a good thing. Despite the valiant efforts of engineers Reg Freeman and Charlie Postles, manning an emergency generator, the waters were winning and the power station was abandoned at 9pm.

By this time some 60 riverside properties in Barbrook and Lynmouth, including two Victorian hotels, were being battered to pieces by a water-borne surge of boulders, trees, telegraph poles, motor cars and the contents of upstream households. Further along the valley, another 32 homes were in an equally parlous state, and a total of 1740 people were in a state of distress ranging from discomfort to being homeless.

Bearded memorial to author Richard Doddridge Blackmore helping church funds at Oare

Across the moor, most people had a better chance of escaping, but bridges were being ripped apart at Exford and Winsford. Even the great stones of the most ancient of all, Tarr Steps, were swept away by the River Barle. Only one of its multiple sections remained intact. Further down the Barle, trees clogged Town Bridge at Dulverton and diverted the rapids through two cottages and the Golden Guernsey Milk Bar. Two vans from Batten and Thorne's yard were washed 7 miles down the valley. The old railway embankment at Parracombe was breached, sweeping sixty-year-old postman William Leaworthy to his death as the River Heddon surged through the village.

Much of the damage could be repaired, over several years, but Lynmouth would never look the same again. The old course of the river became a flood barrier, at Riverside Road, with future waters being provided with a wider course that was cleared through the town. The disaster was a national one as the death toll included three Manchester scouts, who were swept from their tents beside the inappropriately-named Shallowford, on the River Bray at Filleigh. They were Derrick Breddy, Jeffrey Robinson and Harold Shaw. The body of one young woman, a holidaymaker, was never identified. Annual rainfall in a normal year is about 45 inches down in Lynmouth but rises to 90 inches due south on the open ground of the high Chains which were named for challenge they presented to the surveyor's measure.

Traditional latch and catch on the gate between Manor Allotment and South Common

Ancient monuments include the usual Exmoor mix of standing stones and cairns, from the Bronze Age, with a circular Roman fortlet overlooking the coast. This is Old Burrow, half-a-mile north-west of County Gate, which is reached by a track seawards from Black Gate at the western end of Cosgate Hill and the Combe. Old Burrow had tented accommodation, inside an inner square of rampart and ditches, surrounded by circular outer defences. It also served as a signal station and was occupied from AD48 until about AD68 when a larger replacement fort was built, above Martinhoe, with a barracks block for 80 soldiers. Both were abandoned after the Silures tribe in South Wales was subjugated in AD78 and there was no longer any need for patrols in the Bristol Channel to guard against Celtic infiltrators.

THE WALK

The walkers' shelter at County Gate

The best starting point for an exploration is the car park and Visitor Centre beside the A39 at County Gate (SS 793 486). There is a memorial to the *Daily Telegraph* Country Talk contributor John Peel, pre-dating the bearded radio icon, who died in 1983. Set off southwards, through the gate opposite the walkers' shelter, for a 6-mile circuit of Doone Country and Oare. A grassy bridleway follows the fence between the sheep pasture and the eastern wall of the car park. After leaving the stone-banked hedge the track becomes a terrace in the hillside which descends into a double-hedged droveway. Here you join another bridleway beside Oare Water and turn right and then left over the footbridge to walk up through the farmyard to the lane at Malmsmead in half a mile.

Turn right, down to humped-backed Malmsmead Bridge, and cross Badgworthy Water. Then turn left at the junction beside Lorna Doone Farm to follow Post Lane upstream. In 350 yards, at the bend, go through a field gate and follow a bridleway southwards into the heart of Doone Country. Cloud Farm is across the valley to your left in half a mile and you then pass the monolith erected by the Lorna Doone Centenary Committee in 1969 to celebrate Blackmore's novel which 'extols to all the world the joys of Exmoor'.

In another mile, beyond the bewitched wood of mossy and stunted oaks in Yealscombe, you reach the third tributary that pours off the western moors. Turn right here, up the track into Holcombe Combe for 250 yards, into the grassy street of medieval Badgworthy. The best of the ruins is a two-roomed farmstead with stone-walled paddocks on each side. From here, retrace your steps to the Blackmore Memorial and then turn right in 500 yards, across the footbridge, to Cloud Farm.

The onward path turns left, north-eastwards, to pass the sheep pens in another 500 yards and descends into Oare in a further half a mile. Head for St Mary's Parish Church, to the east of the Manor House, and emerge on the road to the right of both the church and the manorial outbuildings.

Turn left to visit the church which also has its Blackmore monument, complete with bearded caricature, and then right at the junction in 50 yards. Follow the lane uphill to New Road Gate, where one of the stone posts is still in situ, in 1200 yards. Turn left at this junction, westwards towards oncoming traffic, to County Gate in a straight and survivable 400 yards.

Pullover time on Stowey Allotment as the flock queues for a photo-call

Embattled tower of the wool-wealth church at Oare

Foreland Point seen from a sea of rosebay willow herb

26

COUNTISBURY AND LYNMOUTH

Devon starts with woods and cliffs east of Lynmouth where the Bristol Channel finally throws off its sickly brown-water overtones of tidal sedimentation and takes on a Mediterranean sparkle. It also boasts extensive National Trust ownership with a network of well-defined paths. Without descending into Lynmouth, these borderlands can be explored from the Exmoor Sandpiper at Countisbury. Southwards, across Trilly Ridge, woods of sessile oaks cover deep-cut slopes around the confluence of the aptly-named Hoar Oak Water with the East Lyn River at Watersmeet. Here, unusually for Exmoor, there are National Trust en route refreshments in Watersmeet House. The summer home of the Halliday family, built in 1830, it was primarily a fishing and shooting lodge.

Next are the first of the dramatic relics and reminders of the great flash-flood of 15 August 1952, which devastated the valley and its twin towns of Lynton and Lynmouth, killing 34 people and making hundreds homeless. The stumps of the washed-away crossing at Bridge Pool have been replaced by Chiselcombe Bridge. Between the oaks, the lush woodlands include Devon whitebeam and mountain ash, with rare Irish spurge beneath, beside luxuriant ferns and mosses in the damper zones.

The River Lyn has been partially tamed but still splits the landscape on its progress to the quay and estuary at Lynmouth. From here you turn east, to climb up and through the cliffside woods to re-enter National Trust land above Black Rocks and Sillery Sands. Defences on Wind Hill range from prehistoric Countisbury Castle to a cannon site and its Second World War successor.

This is a stiff climb up steep slopes – though at least you are not having to push a lifeboat – from sea level to the 850-feet contour. Next are cliff-top Countisbury church and churchyard. In the latter rest most of the heroes, having reached decent old age, of one of the greatest feats in the annals of the lifeboat service in which the Lynmouth rescue boat was hauled across the high moors to Porlock in order to effect an epic rescue. It must have seemed a mission impossible on the night of 12 January 1899. Mountainous seas prevented the launch of the *Louisa* from Lynmouth in aid of the stricken *Forrest Hall*.

The wooded valley of the East Lyn

The Blue Ball Inn resurrected as the Exmoor Sandpiper

Someone pointed out that Porlock Weir lay on the lee side of the hill. Between the two towns lay 12 miles of inadequate road, steep and stony, up which the men and horses hauled their boat, heaving it over obstacles as villagers ran ahead to widen corners and tear out hedges. But the mission was accomplished and the *Louisa* at last went to the aid of the stricken *Forrest Hall*.

THE WALK

The Exmoor Sandpiper Inn, our starting point for this exploration, stands on the south side of the A39, at Countisbury, midway between County Gate and Lynmouth. Park and start in the National Trust car park, which is on the north side of the main road, opposite the inn (SS 747 497).

Set off eastwards, uphill along the main road. Turn right in 100 yards, through the eastern of the two gates. You are now heading south, to Watersmeet, via Trilly Ridge. At the end of the stone-walled track continue straight ahead, keeping the field wall to the left. On reaching the gorse, bear slightly right to head for the tree-covered knoll in the middle distance. A sign points towards the gap in the scrub.

The quay and estuary at Lyn Mouth, from the inspiringly named Eastern Beach

The path passes through the oaks of Horner's Neck Wood and patches of relict heather clumps on defunct anthills across the top of the knoll. From here the track zigzags down the steep wooded slopes towards the sound of Watersmeet. Turn right at the path junction immediately above East Lyn River, as it approaches Hoar Oak Water.

Pass Watersmeet House which is now the National Trust focal point for refreshments and information. Opposite the house is a mine adit, a horizontal shaft, cut in the seventeenth century to extract iron ore. Keep on the east bank of the river after the confluence, bearing right along the track that rises above the water. Look down on Bridge Pool – here are the stumps of the ancient bridge washed away in the 1952 flood, upstream from the replacement stone arch.

National Trust refreshments at Watersmeet House

This is Chiselcombe Bridge, financed by relief fund subscriptions and opened by Earl Fortescue in 1975. The charity tone to the inscription is something of an oddity in that these days one would expect a weather-damaged highway bridge to be automatically restored at public expense. From here there are options – to follow either the woodland or riverside paths – downstream to Lynmouth. The former is to be recommended because the river now turns westwards and its north bank, in the woods, has the best of both the sun and the views. That said, it also tends to be rougher underfoot, as it passes below the scree slopes.

Keep going straight ahead at the path junction in Wester Wood. Our route becomes Arnold's Linhay. A plaque records that the snappily-titled Lynmouth, Lynton and District Association for the Preservation of Local Natural Beauty acquired the central valley for the National Trust in 1936.

Again continue straight ahead, westwards along the north bank of the river, after Woodside Bridge. You arrive in Lynmouth beside the alluring Rocklyn Riverside Tea Garden above the restored river bank in the deep gorge. Follow the river along the road and then the take the footpath beyond Glenville House and Tregonwell Guest House (an intriguing connection with the 'founder' of Bournemouth from 1810). The next section of road leads via the Manor Pleasure Grounds to Rock House and the estuary, opposite the little harbour and quay.

Rocky gorge of the East Lyn on its way into Lynmouth

Here you join the coastal footpath, turning right and eastwards, towards the Foreland and Foreland Point. Turn right at the end of the promenade, along the coast path signed to Minehead. Lynmouth Bay is to the left with Point Perilous projecting. In 20 yards you turn left and then left again at the next path junction, in order to zigzag uphill through

Countisbury church and its mariners' graves

the woods. Keep going uphill, however inviting the alternative. Join the A39 coast road opposite Countisbury Lodge and the car park for the Tors Hotel. Turn left, uphill, along the raised pavement. The retaining wall, a project created to relieve unemployment, is dated 1925 and carries the name Hobbs. You re-enter National Trust land opposite the Beacon Hotel and turn left into it, two yards beyond the Trust's 'Foreland' sign. The coast path heads east, above Sillery Sands and Lynmouth Bay, with Port Talbot opposite. Keep straight ahead, passing below a roadside viewpoint, and then crossing the site of a wartime gun emplacement.

Pass below the outer ramparts of Countisbury Castle outworks. The main Iron Age fortification is further inland on Wind Hill, with great banks across the promontory. Beyond it the path kinks right and then left to follow the stone wall between the bracken and pastures. You are heading north-east along the coast path. On the skyline is a coastguard lookout.

At the end of the walled pastures the walk leaves the long-distance coastal path. Turn right into Countisbury churchyard. Pause and ponder on the graves of the courageous crew of the lifeboat *Louisa*, whose epic feat when recreated a century later could be all the more appreciated. Also note the tower pinnacles of the Parish Church of St John the Evangelist, which are dated 1836 and bear the initials of the churchwarden, R.W.S. Halliday.

From the churchyard, walk down to the gate, and follow the lane southwards to the car park and the Exmoor Sandpiper. Historically, our starting and finishing point was named the Blue Ball Inn, from 1800 to 1986. It then became the Blue Boar, just for one year, and has been the Sandpiper since 1987. Things might have been worse. We could have been concluding our exploration of this wonderful seaboard at the Newt and Lettuce.